Please renew/return this item by the last date shown.

So that your telephone call is charged at local rate,
please call the numbers as set out below: —

	From Area codes 01923 or 0208:	From the rest of Herts:
Renewals:	01923 471373	01438 737373
Enquiries:	01923 471333	01438 737333
Minicom:	01923 471599	01438 737599

L32b

D1549153

The Poetry of Dannie Abse

The Poetry of Dannie Abse

Critical Essays and Reminiscences

Edited and with an Introduction by *Joseph Cohen*

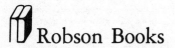 Robson Books

This book is dedicated to my parents, Louis Aaron Cohen and Hattie Klein Cohen, of blessed memory.

Acknowledgments I wish to express my gratitude to Dannie Abse for his willingness to be interviewed and his allowing the authors of the collected essays and myself permission to quote from his poems and plays. I am also grateful to him, and to his wife, Joan, for their hospitality and helpfulness when I visited London in the summer of 1982. For permission to quote from Dannie Abse's poems and his play *Pythagoras*, I express my appreciation to Hutchinson & Co. and to Valentine Mitchell & Co. for use of quotations from *The Dogs of Pavlov*. I am pleased also to express my gratitude to the contributors both for their work and for their enthusiasm and cooperation. Finally, I should like to thank Dr. Ruth S. Samuels for her expert assistance in the editing of the text.

J.C.

FIRST PUBLISHED IN GREAT BRITAIN IN 1983 BY
ROBSON BOOKS LTD., BOLSOVER HOUSE, 5–6 CLIPSTONE STREET,
LONDON W1P 7EB. COPYRIGHT © 1983 ROBSON BOOKS

British Library Cataloguing in Publication Data

Cohen, Joseph
    The poetry of Dannie Abse.
    I. Title
    821'.914   PR6001.B7

    ISBN 0-86051-243-6

Printed in Great Britain by Biddles Ltd., Guildford

Contents

Introduction

The contributors to this collection of essays on Dannie Abse have made my task in introducing their articles both easy and difficult: easy because they have capably identified the essential qualities in Abse's poems and plays and articulated, in many instances superbly, much that is worth knowing about them; difficult because as each contribution arrived it effectively narrowed the range of topics I had anticipated addressing in this space. If, in order to avoid repetition, I have less to say, there is no real loss: I share with the contributors their feelings about the value and impact of Abse's poetry and plays.

Poets with true talents interest us considerably; one who possesses unusual reserves of human warmth becomes especially attractive. This attractiveness can become a problem for an editor. Only editors of *festshriften* can allow a personally affirmative identification with their subject full rein, and this is not a *festschrift*. It is a celebration of sorts, yet one in which an editor anxious to increase the number of readers who share the same appreciation of the writer who is his subject has, nonetheless, to maintain a reasonably objective demeanor and to keep his distance, remembering that however helpful he would be in advancing a particular literary reputation it is, short and long, the burden of the poems and plays themselves which must earn and sustain the literate public's approval.

That Abse's literary works have earned a good deal of public acclaim there is no doubt. He has achieved an unusually high visibility and is in much demand for poetry readings. His volumes of poetry have sold well; he is frequently heard over the radio and occasionally on television; various of his poems and plays, and his early autobiographical novel *Ash On A Young Man's Sleeve* have been translated into foreign languages including Swedish, French, Greek, Polish, Italian, and Hebrew; he has been well received on six reading tours in America; and he is known, too, for his ability as an editor and an author of memorable prose works. A compilation of this kind is, of course, an indicator of public interest.

Yet insofar as public reputations can be accurately measured, Abse's for whatever reason seems not to enjoy the stature which one might have thought would have been assured by his poems and plays. Vernon Scannell is correct when he says that Abse 'has never been awarded the deeply considered evaluation warranted by the seriousness and consistently high quality of his poetry.' Alan Brownjohn, in his informal history of the English poetry scene of the past several decades, touches on the question of reputation in the historical context of the Movement-Mavericks episode of 1956–57, as do Daniel Hoffman and M. L. Rosenthal. Indeed, in my interview with Abse which appears herein, I had hoped to elicit from him a direct statement about what I have taken to be the long-range negative consequences of his opposition to the Movement when he published *Mavericks* in 1957.

The impression I have is that this many years afterward, the Movement-Mavericks issue is largely academic, a historical occurrence of limited interest because neither the Movement nor the Mavericks constituted enduring coteries. Back then, and ever since, Abse has always followed his own bent, and his refusal to identify with this or that group may have more than a little to do with his public acceptance. Had he espoused too long a Maverick (capital M rather than small m) position, automatically swaying to the Movement's dance, that would have become another orthodoxy to oppose. Quiescent, perhaps, in Abse's mind, the question of a kind of historical ostracism is still lively enough elsewhere among the poet's admirers; like a free-floating dice-game, it surfaces where it is least expected, although the game of chance played now has more to do with future than past standings and reputations *vis-a-vis* Abse and Larkin, in terms of the usefulness to the next generations of their very divergent world-views.

This is not a discussion which would engage Abse, or indeed the contributors to this volume, many of whom are great admirers of Philip Larkin's poetry I think it might even make Dannie Abse a little uncomfortable. He has told me more than once of the pleasure that he has from reading Larkin's poetry and of his respect for the poet. The proof of this is to be found in his including pieces by or about Larkin in four of the six *Best of the Poetry Year: Poetry Dimension Annuals* (five if you include Douglas Dunn's 'A Poet in Hull,' 1980), he edited for Jeremy Robson between 1974–1980.

But if Larkin's poetry is representative of the loss of vitality in post-World War II Britain, then Abse's poetry by contrast is noteworthy for its multi-dimensional vision. Larkin's poetry rings true in its providing us with images of a diminished and somewhat shabby Midlands tour through the gray backways of late twentieth-century life; Abse's is no less authentic in its opening of windows from an increasingly cosmopolitan London onto a wider world.

Abse's London, his Golders Green and Soho, his Wales, Cardiff and Ogmore-by-Sea, indeed, his English and Welsh earth, his Jewish heaven and his hospital hell are the topographies whose terrain is surveyed by Jeremy Hooker as well as the aforementioned Scannell, Hoffman and Rosenthal. These essayists, particularly, explore the fruitful tensions growing out of Abse's dualities—one might have been sufficient, but he has at least five—listed by Hoffman as 'British/Jewish, English/Welsh, seeker/skeptic, bourgeois/bohemian, poet/doctor,' the latter duality being marked by the 'deeper division . . . between the scientific objectivity of the physician and the sensibility—introspective, humane—of the poet.' In terms of resources on which to draw, Abse's cup runneth over. I sometimes think that the quiet grumbling over his life in bourgeois Golders Green he occasionally permits himself is actually a pose to keep the gods from ever discovering how fortunate he really is in the kaleidoscopic diversities of his life.

These dualities would of themselves be rich enough if they were the sum total of his *persona*. Within them, however, are satellites, smaller stars and moons, some already discovered, others yet to be charted. One may choose any one-half of a dual equation and explore its manifestations in the Abse cosmos. Take his being Jewish. Opposed to orthodoxy and institutionalism, Abse, regarding himself not uncomfortably as a minimal Jew, is actually a maximal Jew in his private, implacable resistance to the Almighty's boring but deadly insistence on human attrition. Without conscious effort, Abse stands at the heart of Covenantal Judaism. This may be a shock to him, but it is understandable in the terms of Abse's relationship as a Jew to God, a relationship best defined by Karl Shapiro some years ago when he wrote in his *Poems of a Jew* (an interesting compan-

9

ion piece to Abse's *Poems: Golders Green*)' . . . the word *Jew* retains its eternal shock, a shock that has nothing to do with Christ or the Crucifixion. The shock has to do with the Covenant, the intimacy of Jew and God. This intimacy is not sentimental; on the contrary, it is unfriendly. And it is the kind of intimacy that precludes religion itself—for Judaism is the minimum religion—and, secondarily, art itself.'

Whether Covenant is inclusive or exclusive, Abse is increasingly comfortable drawing upon Midrashic and Chasidic sources for his poems. D. J. Enright and John Ormond hint that this attraction may be kabbalistically oriented. They only hint at an Abseian kabbalistic stance but these are hints worth pursuing in the sub-galaxy of Abse's Jewishness. Obviously, the 'non-traditional' tradition, so to speak, in Judaism, would be preferable, to Abse, to the conventional one. You show me a kabbalist and I'll show you a maverick (small m), and any maverick who can pen the line 'God is what that great nothing signifies' ('Sunsets') is closer to Kabbalah than he suspects. The companion piece to 'Sunsets,' 'The Grand View,' further confirms this connection to mysticism in its opening stanzas where the speaker specifically identifies himself not with sleight-of-hand magicians and certainly not with spirit-healers, but with true mystics:

> Mystics, in their far, erotic stance,
> neglect our vulgar catastrophes.
> I, with cadence, rhyme and assonance,
> must pardon their oceanic trance,
> their too saintlike immoralities.
>
> For I, too, spellbound by the grand view,
> flung through vistas from this windy hill,
> am in pure love. I do not know who
> it is that I love, but I would flow
> into One invisible and still.

There is a close connection between Abse's interest in the mysteries of the universe, the emphases placed by mystics on transcendence and miracles, and his recent attraction to Midrashic stories, transformed and skillfully used in 'The Silence of Tudor Evans,' 'Uncle Isidore,' 'Of Rabbi Yose,' 'Snake,' and 'Of Itzig and his dog.' When we add to this connection the explicit gnosticism in the line quoted above from 'Sunsets,' and reflect upon Abse's obsession with the power of evil rampant in the world, also a gnostic undercurrent in Jewish mysticism, we have to acknowledge the possibility that this aspect of Judaism is more central to Abse's world-view than has been previously recognized. It is in this same context, I suspect, that Rosenthal describes Abse as 'our gentlest existentialist,' Hooker says 'he is most memorable when least explicit and most oblique,' and Porter thinks of him in the poet's role of 'purifying the language of the tribe,' for the central concern of the Jewish mystic is to fathom the mystery of Creation by determining the mysterious relationship of language to it. 'I am searching for something forgotten', Abse writes in 'Olfactory Pursuits.'

It could be coincidental, but one begins to wonder when the number of coincidences mount. A kabbalistic interpretation may plausibly be made of another of Abse's poems, his well-known 'A Night Out.' The question posed by the poem is how one responds to the obscenity of Auschwitz. Whatever conventional or traditional, legalistic Judaism advises, kabbalistic tradition is quite explicit. The harmony of the universe is daily facilitated spiritually by sexual congress between God and the *Shekinah*. If an imbalance occurs in the universe and disharmony obtrudes in either the spiritual or the physical world, it will be reflected in the other world. The *Shekinah* withdraws as things anywhere in the cosmos go awry. Humankind, locked into this system of correspondences, is free to be destructive, but it has the responsibility of contributing to the restoration of universal harmony. Physical intercourse, that is, marital love, is an appropriate responsible act. This is the poet's answer to the death-dealing horrors depicted in the movie of the death-camp. The only response to death is life.

There are other aspects to the Jewish dimension of Abse's work. My intention is neither to catalogue them nor to overemphasize this one dimension in Abse's experience; rather, it is to call attention to the worlds within worlds that compose Abse's dualities. This inner multifariousness enriches and deepens Abse's poems. The same multiple effect could be as easily demonstrated for the Welsh dimension or the medical one.

The poems deriving from Abse's experience as a practicing physician are increasingly powerful—the contributors to this collection invoke them continually—and Abse's medical practice is to his poetry, as Hooker and Rosenthal point out, what trench warfare was to Wilfred Owen's poetry. Declarations of war and armistices are merely chronological ciphers in the history books, the wars against human survival go on endlessly, and the combatants are not limited in their choices of uniforms. When I interviewed Abse, I pointed out to him, startling myself, that on the basis of years of investigation into modern war poetry, I had to conclude that an early poem of his, 'Tonight slippers of darkness fall,' was about the worst war poem I had ever read. My opinion of that poem has not changed, but in reading Abse's *Collected Poems* my perspective has been broadened. I think the analogy Hooker and Rosenthal make between Abse's 'Pathology of Colours' and Owen's 'Greater Love' is particularly useful in the light it sheds on the similar methods both poets employ in dealing with human trauma.

One of the tests of true poetry is its flexibility in lending itself to a number of organically-sound interpretations. 'In the theatre,' 'Pathology of colours,' and 'The stethoscope' are examples of medical 'trench' poems which also happen to be spiritual, the latter poem explicitly so.

Beyond their potential for multiple interpretation, Abse's poems are noteworthy also for the variety of forms in which they are cast. From the lyrical mode, Abse swings easily into the narrative and the dramatic modes. Barbara Hardy and D. J. Enright examine Abse's narrative poems, while John Cassidy and Gigliola Sacerdoti Mariani analyze his dramas. The latter like some other essayists here, are attracted to *Funland*, Abse's longest dramatic poem, and to *Pythagoras*, the play which emerged out of it.

In concentrating attention on the poems and the plays, the decision not to invite essays on Abse's novels, or to include commentary on his other prose works, his autobiography, *A Poet in the Family*, and *Medicine on Trial*, or his new collection of autobiographical and critical essays, *A Strong Dose of Myself*, was taken out of the conviction that while these prose works attest to Abse's versatility and breadth, it is primarily his poetry and drama that command our attention.

This decision has seemed sensible in the light of all that could yet be said about the poems and the plays. I shall, however, limit myself to one concluding observation. Throughout this opening statement I have referred to Abse's dualities and to the generally multi-faceted interests of his life that are mirrored in his poetry. In addition to the several previously mentioned, there are others which should at least

12

be recognized. Music, as Peter Porter observes, has frequently provided him not only with subject matter but with total distinctions and effects of sound. Beyond these, I think that the poet's affinity to music has given him a heightened consideration of time, for its winged chariot is never far from the action of any of his poems. Its message is nearly always threatening: in 'The Nameless,' for instance, he speaks of 'certain tunes with their measured malice/that remind us of the dead'; then there are lines such as these from 'Sunday Evening':

> *We, transported by this evening loaded*
> *with a song recorded by Caruso,*
> *recall some other place, another time,*
> *now charmingly outmoded.*
>
> *What, for wrong motives, too often is approved*
> *proves we once existed, becomes mere flattery*
> *—then it's ourselves whom we are listening to,*
> *and, by hearing, we are moved.*
>
> *To know, haunted, this echo too will fade*
> *with fresh alliteration of the leaves,*
> *as more rain, indistinct, drags down the sky*
> *like a sense of gloom mislaid.*

The relationship of music and time to Abse's poetry goes much further than its brief consideration here. My purpose in mentioning it is to emphasize again the versatility present in his poetry.

The collection also includes several essays which focus attention on the poet rather than on his work. When this book was in its initial stages, it became apparent that Abse's personality, his humor, and generosity of spirit would automatically call forth appreciations, reminiscences and other genuine if non-critical responses. Knowing this, my hope was that these commentaries would mirror in celebratory manner that profound humanity which understructures Abse's poems and plays. Donald Davie's 'Grateful Letter to Dannie Abse' is a marvelous example of this kind of response, of reaching out warmly, and of reciprocity, all the more remarkable for the acknowledged differences in their politics and for their determination not to allow those differences to stand between their affirmative consideration of one another. The essays of Theodore Weiss, Alan

Brownjohn and Peter Porter have, to my way of thinking, balanced modesty and the celebratory spirit and are models of good taste, doing honor to their subject, reflecting credit on themselves.

New Orleans, La. May 1983   *Joseph Cohen*

Encounters with Dannie Abse

ALAN BROWNJOHN

It seems to me that it might be possible to write an autobiography in the form of a compendious directory of friends and relations, complete with a system of cross references (incidentally supplying one's personal component of that ever more desirable, so far unattempted, volume, *Who Met Who*). At the head of all the alphabetical entries would necessarily come Dannie Abse. On the bookshelf behind me he is only preceded by the verses of Claude Colleer Abbott, and since that most distinguished Hopkins scholar, and editor of the great volumes of *Letters*, was only the most moderate of poets, that hardly counts. For all practical purposes the slim volumes begin with Dannie's 1948 volume, *After Every Green Thing*.

Does anyone like to have a first book remembered only too vividly? Certainly not, except possibly when it is done in a spirit of celebration: people's recollections of one's excesses of youthful behaviour or conversation are *just* about tolerable at an old college reunion. I should like to celebrate *After Every Green Thing*, briefly, as one of the first volumes by a living poet which I acquired, and hope that its author will not feel embarrassment. It was prised out of the same second-hand shelves, in the same Oxford bookshop, which yielded Roy Fuller's *The Middle of a War*, Spender's *The Still Centre* and a copy of W. H. Auden's *The Dance of Death* with a neat black-ink signature inscribed in it: *Philip Larkin. After Every Green Thing* was written in the free, humane, romantic spirit of 1940s poetry, and as such it spoke to a post-war undergraduate who wanted to know where he might begin with the poetry of his own time.

15

The wisdom of hindsight allows the reader of 1983 to go back and pick up the hints of the later Abse in this first book. Most—well, all—of the imagery we would think of as 'apocalyptic' has now gone. Yet the occasional rhetorical expansiveness, the line that comes at you with a sudden dramatic strength, in the later work, is surely owed to the romantic young poet of *After Every Green Thing*, who could write:

> *When the heads around the table forget to speak* . . .

> . . *They who saw the long unfocussed street,*
> *grinning like a greyhound* . . .

> *the piano-lid closed, a coffin of music* . . .

And a poem like 'Epithalamion,' the version from *Walking under Water*—one which the poet still, rightly, acknowledges—comes into fine shape and sense out of the lyric impulse which (perhaps too undiscriminatingly) flooded the first book.

In an oddly barren literary London of 1953 (*Horizon* and *Penguin New Writing* having been killed off, and *Encounter* and the *London Magazine* not yet started) it was possible, apart from the weeklies (Abse was reviewing for *Time and Tide*) only to find poems printed in a handful of smaller literary magazines. Each one had—in retrospect still *has*—its own kind of fascinating aura. Down in S.W.2 was *Platform*, brainchild of Frederick Woods: substantial, neat, serious, critical. Up in N.W.6. was John Sankey's *The Window*, broad-minded, mildly cosmopolitan, nodding in the direction of the remains of literary Soho, very attractively printed and stitched together. In S.W.3., Blackheath in fact, was the early *Stand*, Jon Silkin's first half-a-dozen numbers providing a small riot of lively graphics and talented poetic unknowns. And from N.W.3. came Dannie Abse's *Poetry and Poverty*. *Poetry and Poverty* was small, compact, relatively plain, sensible in editorial tone, and prestigious. In most magazines it was possible for a new writer to rub shoulders with respected, or envied, peers in one's own age group, as part of a large, loose brotherhood of aspirants. In *Poetry and Poverty* it was sometimes possible to rub shoulders with the distant and the eminent.

There was Jacques Prévert, for example, mellifluously and meticulously translated into English by Paul Dehn; and Paul Célan; and Elias Canetti transcribing an African folk legend—Canetti whose *Auto da Fé* one had been drawn to by a famous commendation of Professor J. Isaacs in a BBC Third Programme lecture, as well as by Stephen Spender's acclaim for a novel he described as a 'long howling crescendo of horror.' All my own copies of *Poetry and Poverty* were borrowed and never returned; the magazine is a rarity now, something no doubt difficult for any editor to believe as he tramps the bookshops of the metropolis distributing small bundles, winning sympathy from some proprietors, weary tolerance from many, contempt and even abuse from a few. My first meeting with Abse, as I recall, was on this kind of pilgrimage. Among the bookshops of the Charing Cross Road, you passed Foyle's, left a few copies of your magazine with the shy, knowledgeable and kindly Ken Fyffe at Better Books, ignored Panzetta's, and stopped with the genial and interested Norman Hart of Zwemmer's before you finished at Collet's. I must have first spoken to Abse when leaving copies of a magazine called *Departure* in Norman's tiny office. He had almost certainly been leaving copies of *Poetry and Poverty*.

It was before the days of the late David Archer's poetry bookshop in Frith Street (a venture which briefly revived the same Parton Press which had first published Dylan Thomas.) It was long before Bernard Stone's Turret bookshops, in Kensington and Covent Garden. There was no London bookshop in which you could unashamedly linger, browse, and not purchase. But you might expect to run into other poets and editors at Better Books and Zwemmer's. How many copies of the little magazines ever sell in the shops (their editors dream of the all-embracing mailing list of subscribers which eliminates the necessity of trudging the streets in the rain, spending more on tube fares than you receive on sales)? And yet their miniature glamour—and their genuine importance—is out of all proportion to their circulation. Part of the glamour of *Poetry and Poverty* was the knowledge that this was a magazine that needed to make its way in a real world of hard-headed London booksellers, not an undergraduate world in which sales are assisted and pride is cushioned by undergraduate esteem. And here was one of the real London editors and poets, leaving copies of his new number.

Was it through Dannie Abse's suggestion, then or at some later point, that I first found my way to the contemporary Mecca of most younger (and a few older) London poets and poetry-readers, virtually the only venue for public readings, the dim, dingy and weirdly haunting basement of the Ethical Church Hall, Bayswater?

17

Someone should, long since, have written a definitive memoir about the readings held under the auspices of the Contemporary Poetry and Music Circle of the Progressive League, at the Ethical Church Hall. Their fame had gone before them: had not Roy Campbell supposedly fought a fist-fight with a famous poet of the 1930s at one reading, had not that and other events been preserved and embellished in more than one novel? Had not everybody of note read there at some time? All the same, they were scanty gatherings (even when after the demolition of the Bayswater hall, they transferred to Stanton Coit House off Kensington High Street, and brought in the likes of Allen Ginsberg and Gregory Corso for their first London appearance.) Ross Nichols had founded the readings, Alec Craig and Ashton Burall had continued them, taking respective responsibility for the poetic and the musical items. Craig and Burall divided the chairmanship of these monthly occasions between them, sitting side-by-side in two very high chairs. It was rumoured that they were not on speaking terms. The events lost money. They were free, but a collection was invited, and the minimum sum asked for once you were in your seats seemed unduly, if understandably, large. The atmosphere was correct and well-ordered, the more outrageous and libertarian material in the programmes being introduced and delivered with a kind of primness derived from the supposition that the atmosphere of an ethical church ought to emulate that of a religious one.

It would have been at one of these two venues of the Contemporary Poetry and Music Circle that I first heard Dannie Abse reading his own work, poems from *Walking Under Water*, and poems which later went into the collection that followed, *Tenants of the House*. Did he read 'Letter to Alex Comfort,' from the first of those two books, on that occasion? Alex Comfort certainly read at Bayswater for Alec Craig, but my memory—perhaps unreliably—puts Abse's reading on another, bitterly cold Monday night late in 1953 when the actor Anthony Jacobs gave a memorial reading of the poems of Dylan Thomas, dead that November. The 'Letter' stayed in my mind from around that time, for the duality it explicitly emphasised in Alex Comfort's concerns—and implicitly suggested in Abse's own:

> *You too, I know, have waited for doors to fly open, played*
> *with your cold chemicals, and written long letters*
> *to the Press; listened to the truth afraid, and dug deep*

> *into the wriggling earth for a rainbow with an*
> *honest spade. . . .*

Did Abse read this one in the gloomy depths of the Ethical Church Hall basement, where so many young poets of the time dug for rainbows? I doubt whether he read the poem actually called 'Duality,' since that came later, I would guess around 1954 or 1955:

> *I am that man twice upon this time:*
> *my two voices sing to make one rhyme.*
> *Death I love and Death I hate,*
> *(I'll be with you soon and late).*

Public poetry reading had not yet undergone that huge expansion of the 1960s, when it became utterly necessary, for authenticity's sake, to have the poet read his or her own work. Sometimes the radio poetry programmes of the time dared to bring in the poets themselves, but mostly they used actors. Anthony Jacobs certainly read my own first broadcast poem, in a Third Programme feature compiled by Jon Silkin in 1955 which also included—in the gifted interpretation of the same reader—Dannie Abse's 'The Victim of Aulis.' It may have seemed to Abse (it certainly seemed to others) one of his most ambitiously moving, yes, rhetorical and expansive, yet controlled and subtle, poems to date. Why he could not read it himself is inexplicable, except in terms of the received wisdom of the day, that poets could not (unless they were Dylan Thomas) read their own poems to any effect; the practice gained by poets in the later poetry reading boom put paid to that impression. Abse read his own work then, as now, with a singular clarity and force, enhanced by a quiet, almost informal delivery. I think of him as one of the poets who convincingly proved that poetry *could* be delivered without some kind of special, reverential voice copied from stage performances, or elocution classes. It is possible that many poets owe the courage to relax vocally in front of an audience to the quieter skills of the radio readers—Anthony Jacobs and Mary O'Farrell then, Hugh Dickson, Gary Watson and Elizabeth Proud now (to name only a few)—who knew better than to address a studio microphone as if it was a theatre auditorium. Abse certainly had the gift.

It was the period when the 1950s 'Movement' in poetry was getting off the ground. The first post-war literary magazine of the

19

air, John Lehmann's *New Soundings*, was succeeded, to its editor's not unjustified disappointment, by John Wain's *First Reading*, which immediately replaced the metropolitan emphasis of its predecessor with gestures of provincial literary defiance. Soon to come were the celebrated 'literary editorials' in the *Spectator*, written by Anthony Hartley and encouraged by one of the best editors of that weekly in the post-war years, Brian Inglis. In reaction against what were held to be the romantic excesses of Dylan Thomas and his followers, the rule of the day for the new poetry was to be emotional coolness, strictness of form, academic wit—the story has often been told, and definitively charted in Blake Morrison's *The Movement*. What has not been so oft or so fully described is the character and origins of the romantic backlash which followed the launching of the Movement. There was an inevitable desire to 'get back' at the new young men of the *Spectator*; even a literary warfare among the weeklies (a *circulation* war conducted by poets and literary editors!) which resulted in counter-claims for its own writers by the long-dead weekly *Truth* (for which wrote the young Alan Brien, Bernard Levin and Philip Oakes). But there was also a conviction that the Movement simply did not represent the bulk, or the best, of the verse being written at the time. Out of that conviction came *Mavericks*.

Mavericks, edited by Dannie Abse and Howard Sergeant, was a counterblast anthology dedicated to proving, with the work of a group of poets parallel in age to the poets of the Movement anthology *New Lines*, that the best writing of the 1950s was *not* sedate, Augustan, a bit bloodless. Like my original copy of *New Lines*, it was lent years ago and never returned, complete with the marginal notes which went into a lecture on the comparative merits of the two volumes, given to a small literary society in West London. *Mavericks* was a good and timely selection, in which the work of Jon Silkin, Vernon Scannell and Dannie Abse himself leaves the most favourable impression in retrospect: and weren't these, with others like Thomas Blackburn, and the co-editor, Howard Sergeant, editor of *Outposts* poetry magazine, the quintessential members of the London little magazine world in the 1950s, a romantic generation who had refined, with the aid of the urbane voice of W. H. Auden, the craft of Thomas, the cadences of W. B. Yeats and George Barker, the 'apocalyptic' poetry of the 1940s to make romanticism acceptable again? As certain members of the Movement (John Wain, Elizabeth Jennings) returned to their romantic instincts, as the poetry of 'the

Group' emerged around the turn of the decade, Ted Hughes achieved a virtually instant celebrity with the publication of *The Hawk in the Rain*, and as Philip Larkin came more and more to seem a poet on whom no easy label could be fixed, so the Movement came to look like an isolated episode (and by this time the *Spectator* had fallen into that bizarre phase when it printed, week after week, *only* the lyrics of Lord Hailsham.) *Mavericks* as well as all the polemic expended in *Truth* and elsewhere, began to seem unnecessary. It had not been so at the time.

But poetry was suddenly emerging from the weeklies and the little literary magazines, and taking to the road. *This* tangled and enthralling stage of literary history undoubtedly requires its annalist, who would be charged with tracing the evolution of poetry in, and as, performance, taking in *New Departures*, Liverpool, the Albert Hall readings of 1965 and 1966— and 'Poetry and Jazz.' There were about three hundred Poetry and Jazz concerts in the middle 1960s, in programmes organised by Jeremy Robson, a number on behalf of Arnold Wesker's Centre 42, with Michael Garrick's quartet. The three I most clearly remember may perhaps serve as a cross section of the efforts of an amazing enterprise. One bitter and misty afternoon the performers took the train to Birmingham to appear in a vast and handsome Victorian music hall, long since demolished in favour of the architectural felicities of the Bull Ring. It sounded, in the pitch darkness out beyond the lights, about half full, but with enthusiasts. Poems were read in the intervals between jazz items, sometimes with *sotto voce* comments from trumpeter Shake Keane or saxophonist Joe Harriott (not audible to the audience), as the jazzmen loyally remained on stage. Books, including Abse's small collection in the 'Pocket Poets' series were sold in the interval—Laurie Lee, on stage, held up his, proclaiming it as the 'life's work' of a slow writer. There followed a nightmare return journey, made, for some reason, in a minibus with erratic brakes, in thick motorway fog.

On a second night the wholly untypical venue was the Council Chamber at Southall. It was full, but only with the numbers required to fill it with councillors, so that the large-looking audience really consisted of about fifty persons. On a third evening the big Colston Hall in Bristol was filled to capacity, justifying the theory that the different followings, for words and for music, would complement each other and create large popular audiences for the right combination of the two. At this stage—I suppose some time early in 1964—only one poet had the daring to combine the poetry with the music: Jeremy Robson. But he later persuaded John Smith, Vernon Scannell and even Thomas Blackburn to make the attempt. Jeremy Robson I felt to be the organising spirit behind Poetry and Jazz, Dannie Abse (and with the jazz musician, Michael Garrick, who would expound his latest musical and philosophical theories and hopes late at night in motorway restaurants) the stabilising force, whose calm, and common-sense, held a collection of wayward spirits together through several touring years. As a result, 'Poetry and Jazz in Concert' found—or created—its own very special kind of audience, one which cared to listen to words, celebrate jazz, and connect with the craft in both. I doubt whether this has happened since in the purlieus of popular music. There ought to have been more than just two gramophone records of the group; and some lines on the evocative character of recorded sound, in this case Caruso, in an Abse poem read at some of the concerts, seem to offer an appropriate nostalgia:

> *Dear classic, melodic absences*
> *how stringently debarred, kept out of mind,*
> *till some genius on a gramophone*
> *holes defences, breaks all fences.*
>
> *What lives in a man and calls him back*
> *and back. . .?*

I first recall hearing many of the poems in Abse's next two volumes, *Poems Golders Green* and *A Small Desperation* in the various reading venues that had sprung up in the London of the mid-1960s: places like the Crown and Greyhound, Dulwich Village (which had a reputation among poets for somewhat chilling, poker-faced audiences), the Questors Theatre (for which Abse was writing plays), the Regent's Park Library, where Elizabeth Thomas chaired the many *Tribune* readings with unflappable ease and authority, and the numerous pubs, clubs and halls where happened the more short-lived reading-series put together by organisers with rather less stamina or manic enthusiasm. In 1967 there was to be a couple of Arts Council Poets' Tours organised by the present writer; one trio of poets, John Holloway, Patric Dickinson and Edward Lucie-Smith, was to go east from London into Essex and Suffolk, and another westwards, to Oxfordshire and Gloucestershire: Dannie Abse, Vernon Scannell and Elizabeth Jennings. The eastern group suffered nothing worse (though that was bad enough) than the theft of Patric's suitcase in the vicinity of a London public school. Two days before the western group was due to set out, Vernon Scannell—in circumstances described fully in his book *A Proper Gentleman*—was sent to Brixton Prison. The first afternoon in the west, a reading at Cheltenham Ladies' College, therefore featured a reading by Dannie Abse, Elizabeth Jennings and Michael Hamburger. I drove Elizabeth Jennings from Oxford to Cheltenham; Dannie Abse drove the trio on, for four days, to places like Gloucester and Bicester, a school to read in, in the afternoons, a library in the evenings.

I think of this tour, or perhaps more exactly this year of 1967, as the time when I first became aware of the poems which went to make Abse's *A Small Desperation*. 'As I was saying' (and indeed 'Not Adlestrop') connects inseparably for me with the landscape of Gloucestershire and the high public library hall where I first heard it, a poem in which the gentler face of 1940s romanticism shades into Edward Thomas and Philip Larkin, suddenly assembling evidence of an English tradition which one hadn't previously noticed in three apparently different poets; the subject is wild flowers:

> *which is this one and which that one,*
> *what honours the high cornfield, what the low water,*
> *under the slow-pacing clouds and occasional sun*
> *of England.*

Other poems in *A Small Desperation*, not coincidentally in the period of the Vietnam war, have that dimension of unease, of alarm lurking just under the surface, which Abse has continued to explore more and more successfully and movingly. It surfaces overtly in the *Funland* sequence, in the book of that title, and I have to say I like it less in that explicit form than in the more menacing, *because* more indistinct, form it takes in poems like 'The Sheds,' which has haunted me since I first heard it:

> *Articulate suffering may be a self-admiring,*
> *but what of the long sheds where a man could only howl?*
> *How quickly, then, silhouettes came running*
> *across the evening fields, knee deep in mist.*

> *Or what of nights when the sheds disappeared,*
> *fields empty, a night landscape unrhetorical*
> *until the moon, pale as pain, holed a cloud?*
> *As if men slept, dreamed, as others touched on lights.*

One writes 'heard' almost without thinking. In the 1960s and early 1970s the experience of sharing reading platforms with other poets meant that the new work of friends might be as frequently met in that setting as in print in magazines: heard as you sit wondering what on earth you are going to start with yourself when it is your turn to read, or wondering just what kind of impression you have made when you've just sat down after delivering. These are conditions in which a poem has to possess some unmistakeable, immediately recognisable force in order to 'come through.' 'Hunt the thimble' seemed the genuine article, as did 'Fah', the one about the single, repeated note sounded on a piano:

> *that one sound, at first amiable,*
> *soon touched down on the whole feminine,*
> *far world of hermetic lamentations.*
> *You sat there, it seemed, absent, unaware,*
> *like a child (certainly without menace)*
> *and fathomed it again and played it again,*
> *a small desperation this side of death.*

Some poems settle into the corners of the memory, tacitly offering their themes for emulation; only after several attempts to write a wholly serious poem about the strangely evocative sound of someone idly fingering a musical instrument did I remember that 'Fah' had done the idea conclusively, and content myself with writing an inferior comic one.

If you engage in the activity of reviewing you find your own encomia coming back at you from the dust-jackets of shiny new volumes, recalling the dash for the deadline, the elimination of printers' solecisms from the proofs, the last-second sub-editing which has reduced an immaculate bit of delicate critical syntax to a half-sentence of terse gibberish. On the back of *Funland* I see that I wrote in the *New Statesman* about Abse's *Selected Poems* that 'Dannie Abse's new volume . . . (*dot dot dot*: what piece of inspired parenthetical elaboration has been excised?) shows a remarkable unity of theme and method in twenty years' work . . . (This time my own dots). Abse is talking quietly and persuasively to people who will understand, listen and agree. At his very best he uses this warmth and approachableness to lead the reader on to accept some disquieting, original and memorable effects.' You don't invariably feel, especially after the passage of a few years, as if you want to stand by what you wrote just before the Literary Editor rang to demand his copy. I would certainly stand by that statement from 1973, ten years ago—and take it further if I was asked to write it again. In the 1980s, the dust has settled after the wild, raw, demonstrative, sloganising poetry that made news in the sixties and seventies. But it has settled too much, too solidly, and shaped a consensus that poetry should preferably be a decorative whimsical art, only disquieting if it arbitrarily chooses to invert the ordinary world in which people actually live, work, hope and starve to serve the cause of private fantasies. I like to think that one function of poetry is to lead you quietly and unnervingly towards inescapable human truths. And I dare to believe that Dannie Abse will go on writing poems of that kind.

A Vision of the Street

VERNON SCANNELL

The vacillations of literary reputation and fashion, especially among poets and poetry, are a curiosity of history, and those of the final quarter of the 20th Century will no doubt seem as strange to posterity—provided, of course, that there is to be a posterity, and that it will be a literate one—as any of the evaluative oddities of the past. Looking back at what seem now to be the misjudgements of the critics of former times—the high estimate for example, of the poetry of Nicholas Rowe, whose translation of Lucan (1718) was, according to Johnson, 'one of the greatest productions of English poetry,' the admiration expressed by Coleridge and Wordsworth for the sonnets of William Lisle Bowles, the immense popularity of Sir Lewis Morris, the office of Poet Laureate awarded to Alfred Austin and William Watson's knighthood, to mention only a few—what appears to be at fault was less a matter of perverted or imprecise critical principles as a failure properly to apply criteria which were, in themselves, perfectly sound. What seems to be to be wrong with a great deal of contemporary criticism is that the very bases from which judgements proceed are either set in shifting quicksands of uncertainty or upon more solid but narrow and lopsided foundations. The critics of the past, many, if not most, of whom were themselves fine poets, knew what it was that they valued in poetry: the anonymous admirer of Chaucer who wrote the following lines set down a simple list of desiderata for poetic excellence which could serve as a foundation for all future criticism until the post-modernist 20th Century:

Redith his werkis ful of plesaunce
Clere in sentence in langage excellent
Briefly to write suche was his suffysance
Whatever to saye he toke in his entente
His langage was so fayr and pertynente
It seemeth unto mannys heerynge
Not only the worde but verely the thynge.

There we have the demands for clarity and economy of expression, compression and the ability to present the thing itself, the image; but before these comes the primary requirement, that the work should be 'ful of plesauance,' the power to give pleasure, and it is this first principle that has been either ignored or subverted by so much of the more influential criticism of the past half-century.

The pleasure that a reader will receive from poetry is dependent on those qualities of 'fayr and pertinente' language which has the power to present 'verely the thynge.' Pleasure, of course, is a private experience and one which we have no way of quantifying. It is its elusively subjective nature which has led the quasi-scientific puritans of Structuralism and Deconstructionism to dismiss it as a sentimental irrelevance in any discussion of literary values, but in fact it is the only practical guide to artistic excellence; if we receive no initial pleasure or promise of future pleasure from a work of art it will have nothing else to offer us. Poetry, Dr Johnson said, is the 'art of uniting pleasure with truth by calling imagination to the aid of reason' and it is the poetry which most effectively fulfills this definition which I value above other, more pretentious kinds of writing.

Among the highly regarded poetic reputations of today some seem to me well-deserved, others less so but established for reasons which can be discerned and understood, if not endorsed, while the rest appear to be either quite inexplicable or achieved by means that have little to do with the art of literature. That there are some untalented scribblers enjoying fame and perhaps even a little material gain from their undeserved reputations as poets does not worry me nearly as much as the fact that there are a few truly gifted poets writing admirable and enjoyable work which receives comparatively small critical recognition and, among those is one who, while being given respectful notices in the literary press, has never been awarded the deeply considered evaluation warranted by the seriousness and consistently high quality of his poetry. This is Dannie Abse, a poet who has been publishing verse since the late 1940s and the publication of whose *Collected Poems* in 1977 should have provided the occasion for such thorough consideration.

A first reading of the *Collected Poems* yields an overriding impression of consistency: from the earliest poems to the last there are very few occasions when the primary expectations of pleasurable readability, formal accomplishment, honesty and clarity of expression are disappointed. The personality which emerges from these poems is an unusual and engaging one which shows a deep humanistic concern for suffering and injustice allied to a religious instinct which is counterbalanced by a shrewdness and a comic sense that steer Abse away from the pitfalls of sentimentality. His religious sense seems to be not specifically Jewish or Christian but draws nourishment from both faiths, finding sustenance in the mythopoeic or allegorical rather than in the doctrinal features of each: it functions in a searching, heuristic way rather than in liturgical or devotional forms, in a determination to seek and find beneath the shifting surfaces of quotidian existence the permanent and truly valuable.

In a short, early poem called '*The Moment*' from *Tenants of the House* (1957). Abse depicts one of those tiny domestic episodes, that everyone can recognize and identify with, and he probes beneath the ordinariness to find the mystery and the significance.

> *You raise your eyes from the level book*
> *as if deeply listening. You are further than I call.*
> *Like Eurydice you wear a hurt and absent look,*
> *but I'm gentle for the silence into which you fall*
> *so sadly.*
> What are you thinking? Do you love me?
> *Suddenly you are not you at all but a ghost*
> *dreaming of a castle to haunt or a heavy garden;*
> *some place eerie, and far from me. But now a door*
> *is banging outside, so you turn your head surprised.*
>
> *You speak my name and someone else has died.*

The first sentence is very simple and direct and its truthfulness is crucial to the poem. That superficially off-hand simile, 'as if deeply listening,' is very effective both visually and semantically. The reader at once sees the woman held in that posture of still, almost breathless attentiveness, looking up from the book, gazing into space. But 'deeply listening' contains the possibility that she might indeed be listening for some distant sound or voice. The exactness and authenticity of the opening image invest all that follows with the same persuasiveness: the truth of the physical is carried over into the metaphysical. The poem is a celebration of the extraordinariness of the commonplace. The 'moment' of the title is one which all of us have experienced, that unnerving realisation that each of us is the lonely inhabitant of a world closed to all others, even those nearest to us in the bonds of love and familial circumstance. The 'someone else' that has died as the woman speaks is the unreachable, unknowable someone she had, for the rapt, dangerous moment become.

The form of the poem shows the unobtrusive craftsmanship which distinguished Abse's work almost from the start. The rhythmic movement of his lines is always very close to the natural cadences of common speech yet it is usually founded on a patterning which may at any moment be sharpened to accommodate a muted lyricism. In 'The Moment' the lines vary between four and five stresses of sprung rhythm and the rhymes, slant rhymes and assonances are placed irregularly so that the chimes are often unexpected and teasingly effective. In the first four lines, for example, the ear is both satisfied yet surprised by the rhyme for *call* occurring on the penultimate stress of *fall* which is followed by the feminine *sadly*, echoed at the end of the next line in *love me*. Then, in the sixth line that *call* and *fall* rhyme is gently chimed again in 'you are not you at *all*'; from then, until the final couplet, end-rhyme is not used and this avoidance of the predictability of conventional rhyming not only helps to give the poem its feeling of authentic experience but the pattern of echoes reflects the teasing, half-familiar nature of the event itself.

'The Moment' is one of Abse's relatively slight poems but it shows the same care, the same thoughtful structuring of the verbal pattern to mirror as closely as possible the shape of the experience as is exhibited in his more ambitious pieces. And it shows, too, that even with this poet's slighter works the reader is never shortchanged, he is always given the real thing. At a time when so many pieces of writing possessing the rhythmic vitality and verbal radiance of the instructions for a puncture repair-kit are solemnly applauded as major poetry it is unusually refreshing to encounter the work of a poet who seems never to commit words to the page unless he is truly compelled, whose every poem possesses at least the interest of a splinter of recognizable human experience being minutely, deeply and honestly examined and mirrored in language the texture, sense and sound of which are calculated to surprise and delight.

Dannie Abse is an urban poet, one might almost say 'metropolitan' since the action and furnishings of many of his poems are set in London, but his use of locus and imagery is always more than purely topographical: certainly he is sensitive to and very much concerned with communicating that oddly exciting and haunting poetry of the great city, its streets, pubs, cafes, suburbs and assorted denizens, but the objects and creatures, while retaining their own sharply observed distinctiveness, lead to deeper and more mysterious areas and presences, towards '. . . a vision of the street/As the street hardly understands.' A simple instance of this is to be found in his 'Three Street Musicians' (*Funland and Other Poems*, 1973) where the sharply realised picture of the buskers progresses first to a meditation on the power of old popular tunes to stir memories and raise phantoms from the past and finally to an extraordinary conflation of images of the city street and the risen ghosts of memory.

Three Street Musicians

Three street musicians in mourning overcoats
worn too long, shake money boxes this morning,
then, afterwards, play their suicide notes.

The violinist in chic, black spectacles, blind,
the stout tenor with a fake Napoleon stance,
and the loony flautist following behind,

they try to importune us, the busy living,
who hear melodic snatches of music hall
above unceasing waterfalls of traffic.

Yet if anything can summon back the dead
it is the old-time sound, old obstinate tunes,
such as they achingly render and suspend:

'The Minstrel Boy,' 'Roses of Picardy.'
No wonder cemeteries are full of silences
and stones keep down the dead that they defend.

Stones too light! Airs irresistible!
Even a dog listens, one paw raised, while the stout,
loud man amazes with nostalgic notes—though half boozed

and half clapped out. And, as breadcrumbs thrown
on the ground charm sparrows down from nowhere,
now suddenly, there are too many ghosts about.

As in 'The Moment' Abse deploys his rhymes cunningly, not only placing them before the end-line stress as in the third stanza—*music hall* and *waterfall*—but using them to sew stanzas together as *suspend* and *defend* link stanzas 4 and 5 and *stout* and *about* the final two. The poet signals at once, in the first sentence, that we are watching something other than a simple street scene: the overcoats are 'mourning', they are black. They are melancholy but are they not, too, literally garments of grieving? The punning 'suicide notes' answers that question. The coats are 'worn too long,' they are of an unfashionable length, but we are aware of the other sense of the musicians having worn them for too long a period. In stanza three, the 'busy living' are contrasted with the musicians who themselves become unnervingly spectral. The whole poem is both lucid and mysterious and it is this quality of contrapuntal clarity and mystery that Abse develops so fruitfully throughout his work.

I should like to glance here at two shorter poems where this quality is, in different ways, shown at its most effective before attempting a brief examination of what must be one of his most ambitious and interesting single works, the longer poem, *Funland*.

'Hunt the Thimble' is one of a number of poems in *A Small Desperation* (1968) in which elusively vagrant perceptions, often sensory ones, are seized and investigated for the significance they so tantalizingly hint at. In 'Olfactory Pursuits' the poet deals with the smell of his own hand, in 'Halls' the smell in the halls of urban or suburban houses; in 'Pathology of Colours' various hues are invoked and seen manifest in, and emblematic of situations of pain and death. 'Hunt the Thimble' brilliantly takes the childhood game for an extended metaphor of search. Any attempt to provide a precise prose account of the meaning of this poem would be absurdly self-defeating. The mystery which is the poet's subject cannot be defined, it can only be invoked or enacted through images. It is the secret that we all want to know, the ultimate mystery of life and death and what lies beyond both.

The poem is a dialogue or catechism: one voice is of the questioning, limited human intelligence supported by brief flashes of imagination, the voice of the poet, and the other, answering voice is anonymous, omniscient perhaps, but not prepared to reveal all its owner understands. The poem begins with these words from the second voice:

> 'Hush now. You cannot describe it'

But the questioner will not accept the ineffable. He insists on attempting to define, by comparison with the known, the unknowable and indefinable. The answering voice replies each time with the discouraging 'Hunt the Thimble' reply of 'Cold.' The comparisons invoked as first by the seeker are images of generalised melancholy.

> Is it like heavy rain falling,
> and lights going on, across the fields,
> in the new housing estate?
>
> . . . dark windowed street at night,
> the houses uncurtained, the street deserted?
>
> The brooding darkness then,
> that breeds inside a cathedral
> of a provincial town in Spain?

Then there is a brief upsurge of optimism, but the deliberate banality of the image betrays lack of conviction:

> Aha—the blue sky over Ampourias,
> The blue sky over Lancashire for that matter . . .

And then back to similes of a melancholy now more specifically generated by the fear of death. The omniscient voice is parentally and perfunctorily consoling but still offers no answer and after the wonderfully resonant and desolating image of the nothingness attendant on mortality—'the darkness inside a dead man's mouth'—the 'cold' in the response become unequivocally the coldness of death.

Here is the poem in its entirety:

32

Hunt the Thimble

Hush now. You cannot describe it.

Is it like heavy rain falling,
and lights going on, across the fields,
in the new housing estate?

Cold, cold. Too domestic, too
temperate, too devoid of history.

Is it like a dark windowed street at night,
the houses uncurtained, the street deserted?
Colder. You are getting colder,
and too romantic, too dream-like.
You cannot describe it.

The brooding darkness then,
that breeds inside a cathedral
of a provincial town in Spain?

In Spain, also, but not Spanish.
In England, if you like, but not English.
It remains, even when obscure, perpetually.
Aged, but ageless, you cannot describe it.
No, you are cold, altogether too cold.

Aha—the blue sky over Ampourias,
the blue sky over Lancashire for that matter . . .

You cannot describe it.

. . . obscured by clouds?
I must know what you mean.

Hush, hush.

Like those old men in hospital dying,
who, unaware strangers stand around their bed,
stare obscurely, for a long moment,
at one of their own hands raised—
which perhaps is bigger than the moon again—
and then, drowsy, wandering, shout out, 'Mama.'

Is it like that? Or hours after that even:
the darkness inside a dead man's mouth?

> *No, no, I have told you:*
> *you are cold, and you cannot describe it.*

The other short poem, 'The Stethoscope,' is less exploratory than
'Hunt the Thimble,' in other words I suspect that here the poet had
a more definite notion of the conclusion to which the poem would
lead him than in the inevitably irresolute enquiry of the poem we
have just looked at. Nevertheless, it does offer that sense of mystery
at the heart of its lucidity which characterises Abse's best work and
it contains a similarly powerful rhetoric which paradoxically is
achieved through a deliberate avoidance of the vocabulary of conventional rhetoric. A line like 'the darkness inside a dead man's mouth'
pierces to the marrow, but it does not do so by the means that
Wordsworth, for instance, employs in 'Resolution and Independence,' when he writes 'And mighty Poets in their misery dead' for
here each key word, even in isolation, is charged with rich emotive
associations and the music of the line is symphonic. Abse's line is
rhythmically conversational and its power derives from the unexpected conjunction or dislocation of ordinary things: 'darkness' is
not usually associated with the inside of the human mouth: once the
connection is made the mouth becomes a cave, a thing of stone,
stone-dead.

In 'The Stethoscope' Abse speaks of hearing '. . . in a dead man's
chest, the silence/before creation began.' Again the separate words
are not—perhaps excepting 'dead' and 'creation'—especially evocative through association or sound, and in fact that 'dead man's chest'
might summon unwanted, risible, echoes of piratical yo-ho-hoing.
But of course it does no such thing, counterpointed as it is against
the image of the stirring of new life in the womb of a young woman
and the rare *frisson* of poetic awe is powerfully transmitted. The
poem uses the stethoscope as both physical object and emblem
representing any instrument which enables man to investigate areas
of knowledge from which he might otherwise be excluded, but the
poet is well aware of the danger of attempting to establish science as
a religion He asks:

> *Should I*
> *kneel before it, chant an apophthegm*
> *from a small text? Mimic priest or rabbi,*
> *the swaying noise of religious men?*
> *Never! Yet I could praise it.*

He would praise it; he goes on to explain, because he would 'by doing so celebrate my own ears'; the poem which seemed to begin as a celebration of scientific achievement ends in lyrical affirmation of the human:

> *night cries*
> *of injured creatures, wide-eyed or blind;*
> *moonlight sonatas on a needle;*
> *lovers with doves in their throats; the wind*
> *travelling from where it began.*

And, again, in that final image of the wind's source and the source of all creation we hear the strangely vibrant rhetoric of plain and reticent speech after the more fanciful conceits and verbal arabesques which precede it.

In 'The Smile Was' (*A Small Desperation*) Abse attempted a poem of some substance which would be a statement of affirmation and celebration, a work which would call upon his experience as a medical practitioner and while facing the inescapable truths of the human predicament, birth and death, hope and fear, suffering and ecstasy, be in its final effect resoundingly on the side of life. Despite its incidental felicities I cannot regard this poem as a complete success: it is, I feel, too schematic and too explicit in its conclusions. The smile of the title is that which, according to the poem, is seen upon the face of every new mother whether she be

> *Whore, beauty, or bitch*
> *it makes no odds*
> *illimitable chaste happiness*
> *in that smile. . .*

Here I find a strident rhetoric unlike that of 'Hunt the Thimble' and 'The Stethoscope', a conjunction of words—*Whore, beauty, bitch, happiness*—each of which separately carries too rich charge of association and meaning for their combination to work comfortably. The effect is excessive: the reader is more likely to be embarrassed than moved.

'The Smile Was' is written in four parts, the first a vivid account of the drama of natural human birth followed by a meditation on the mother's smile on hearing for the first time her baby's cry; the second, a curiously chatty, anecdotal strophe telling the story of an

Indian patient of the poet-doctor who was convinced, despite all assurances to the contrary that he was dying: this ends with his fatalistic smile being contrasted with the archetypal smile of the new mother. In the third section the smile of a surgeon, described in terms which suggest that Abse accepts, at least in this case, the Freudian notion of the surgeon as a sublimated Ripper, provides the comparison and, finally, the poem ends with a rhetorical coda again celebrating the universal post-natal smile of woman.

Despite its failure properly to cohere into a unified structure and its occasional stridencies of tone 'The Smile Was' is important in that it served as a kind of bridge leading the poet from territory that he had most resourcefully and fruitfully explored into the more difficult terrain of the longer reflective, philosophical poem, towards in fact the almost unqualified success of 'Funland.' In this poem Abse adopts a strategy of obliquity, a strangely surrealist method of investigating, not the private grounds of subjective experience but no less than the predicament of mankind itself, or, rather, what is called 'civilization,' in the second half of the 20th Century. It is an audacious and remarkably successful attempt to project a vision of a disintegrating or terribly threatened world and it bears some resemblance to that earlier poetic vision of the modern Western world in decay, *The Waste Land*. There are, in fact, a few small genuflexions to the Master, as in section 3, 'The Summer Conference' in which the lines 'Why should the agèd eagle stretch its wings?' (*Ash Wednesday*) and the references to the superintendent in section 6, 'Autumn in Funland,' as a 'ruined millionaire' who '. . . will not dress a wound even' echoes—equally deliberately I imagine—the fourth part of *East Coker*. But this is not to suggest that 'Funland' is in any sense derivative or imitative. I know of no other poem which offers quite the same strange but wholly effective mixture of the bizarre, dreamlike and comic, the speculative, lyrical and satirical.

The poem is constructed in nine interrelated sections in which an assortment of characters make their appearances, the superintendent, the narrator's atheist uncle, fat Blondie, the man nicknamed Pythagoras, and Mr Poet. Each of these characters possesses an allegorical or symbolic significance just as Funland itself, institution for the deranged, surrealist nightmare and the world we inhabit, exists on various planes. But the poem as a whole resists a too precise interpretation of each element. Much of its power to please and disturb proceeds from the shimmering, slightly unfocused view presented, from the sense of the mysterious, the menacing and the absurd which is strengthened by the causes being only partially revealed. Mr Poet's public reading in Section 4 consists of the repeated howling of a couple of obscene monosyllables: art, or what passes in this mad-house for art, can offer neither explanation nor consolation. Science, religion, human love are found to be insufficient. The Superintendent dies and the narrator's atheist uncle takes uncertain command, proclaiming that he is immortal. Towards the end Pythagoras, the gentle philosopher of numbers and silence, the legendary inventor of the lyre, has been executed and the narrator says:

> And I? I write a letter to someone nameless
> in white ink on white paper
> to an address unknown.
> Oh love I write
> surely love was no less
> because less uttered or more accepted?
>
> My bowels are made of glass.
> The western skies try to rouge the snow.
> I goosestep across this junk of heaven
> to post my blank envelope.
>
> Slowly night begins in the corner
> where two walls meet.
> The cold is on the crocus.
> Snows mush and melt
> and small lights fall from twigs.
>
> Bright argus-eyed the thornbush.
>
> Approaching the pillar box
> I hear its slit of darkness screaming.

Then in the ninth and final section we are given an apocalyptic glimpse of the 'abyss,' of the nothingness that has been threatening from the start to overwhelm Funland. The whole poem takes a decidedly bleak look at the Western world at the present time, and its only answer to, or possible remedy for, the engulfing horror that advances ever closer is itself, its wit, sprightliness, courage and vision, its faith in the imagination's power to move mountains.

Way Out in the Centre (1981), Dannie Abse's one collection since the publication of the *Collected Poems*, provides solid proof that his talent is still developing. It contains nothing so ambitious as 'Funland' but all of the poems are fashioned with a strength and delicacy that will last and some of the short moral tales carry a curiously timeless quality, a sense of hard-won wisdom, effortlessly and gracefully communicated, that will surely gain for them a place in any conservatory of the best and most enjoyable literature of our time.

Dannie Abse: Gentle Existentialist

M. L. ROSENTHAL

The plain humanity of Dannie Abse's poetry is one of its attractive qualities. He speaks entirely as a domesticated city man—married, a father, with a profession (medicine), rather Left politically, but too decent and compassionate to contemplate violence really. And his background has kept him—London householder though he has been for these many years—from a complacent or a tatty insularity. He was born in Wales, but doubly saved from the provincialism that circumstance might have led to by his Jewish parentage and by his willy-nilly membership in the semi-bohemian companionship of the British theatre and, of course, of his fellow poets. And he is a good soul—not an ounce of the literary or academic backbiter in the man—with a wife (Joan Abse) whose own intelligence and literary skills are a pleasure (for him as for the rest of us) to behold.

In short, he is a normal modern man of sensibility living the good life despite the usual problems, including an all too normal income, most of us must face. His genius isn't a mad one; he's not a Lowell—and wouldn't capitalize on his private maladies if he were. There isn't a trace of the misogynist, or the region-proud Little Englander or archaeology-hip élitist or macho vampire or Willy-Wetleg-Weeping-Over-Its-Woeful-Childhood about him. And yet he is one of the true poets of the age and his work connects directly with what one whole tendency of British poetry embodies: a genuine, humane, yet tough-enough-minded, self-questioning civilization. The civilization is quietly, sanely European, with a touch perhaps of the kind of openness one might associate with the American mind when it is behaving itself. All this is part and parcel of Abse's poetry.

39

If anyone supposes I've been describing a rather unpoetic personality, let him or her think again. It's just that Dannie Abse is one of us (as Keats would have been). The daily streets of our twentieth-century lives are his streets too. On them he moves sensitively but unpresumptuously amid the traffic and the hopes, the heart-sickening memory of the Holocaust and the old idiocies of the new governments, thinking and feeling his kindhearted, sometimes anguished, often bemused and wondering way through routines that can amaze him. Meanwhile, his poetry connects with the life we know and with a tradition of modern poetry that speaks naturally in a mode developed by many poets since Wordsworth, including Hardy, Edward Thomas, and Auden. Abse's 'Not Adlestrop,' for instance, is a sort of curious conversation with Thomas's poem 'Adlestrop,' which goes (you remember):

> Yes, I remember Adlestrop—
> The name, because one afternoon
> Of heat the express-train drew up there
> Unwontedly. It was late June.
>
> The steam hissed. Someone cleared his throat.
> No one left and no one came
> On the bare platform. What I saw
> Was Adlestrop—only the name
>
> And willows, willow-herb, and grass,
> And meadowsweet, and haycocks dry,
> No whit less still and lonely fair
> Than the high cloudlets in the sky.
>
> And for that minute a blackbird sang
> Close by, and round him, mistier,
> Farther and farther, all the birds
> Of Oxfordshire and Gloucestershire.

'Adlestrop' develops slowly and quietly; not until the third stanza do we meet inversions and the sudden emergence of pastoral lyricism. Then, in the final stanza, the poem bursts into two kinds of Hardyesque music, somehow recalling the quixotic bird of 'The Darkling Thrush' and, in the closing line, the ending of 'Channel Fire.'

Compare 'Not Adlestrop,' written by Abse a half-century later (about 1965) and sounding a little as though D. H. Lawrence had helped:

> Not Adlestrop, no—besides, the name
> hardly matters. Nor did I languish in June heat.
> Simply, I stood, too early, on the empty platform,
> and the wrong train came in slowly, surprised, stopped.
> Directly facing me, from a window,
> a very, very, pretty girl leaned out.
>
> When I, all instinct,
> stared at her, she, all instinct, inclined her head away
> as if she'd divined the much married life in me,
> or as if she might spot, up platform,
> some unlikely familiar.
>
> For my part, under the clock, I continued
> my scrutiny with unmitigated pleasure.
> And she knew it, she certainly knew it, and would not
> glance at me in the silence of not Adlestrop.
>
> Only when the train heaved noisily, only
> when it jolted, when it slid away, only then,
> daring and secure, she smiled back at my smile,
> and I, daring and secure, waved back at her waving.
> And so it was, all the way down the hurrying platform
> as the train gathered atrocious speed
> towards Oxfordshire or Gloucestershire.

Thomas's quatrains, with their simple meter and rhyme-scheme (each significantly varied only once—the meter in the breath-caught, exquisite eleventh line; the rhyme in the closing line—but to beautiful effect) swell into pure music. Offhand realism, unromantic understatement, become transmuted (were it not for the time of day) into a medieval *aubade*, chorus of birds and all. Abse's free-verse lines begin as a kind of joke, as if he were having a conversation with a good friend—with Thomas, in fact—and telling about an experience that reminded him of the friend's poem. This sort of conversation does often occur in a pleasing way between poets who have some regard for one another's work. It happens among contemporaries who actually do know and speak with one another; and it happens—as here—over the years in imagination

41

only, when a poet has absorbed a forerunner's writings into his or her own soul and then holds imagined converse with them. This is influence in the best sense—lovingly received and dealt with, like mother's milk and father's confirming presence. (Or, to step back from unintended Freudian suggestions, it is like the mannerisms and attitudes friends pick up from one another and absorb into their own characters. The way that Thomas and Robert Frost affected each other's verse makes a perfect instance.)

At any rate, Abse echoes Thomas's initial tone in a series of negatives that distinguish what he's about from that moment of something like anomie at the start of 'Adlestrop.' And there's a touch of that same anomie in Abse's first lines too; but at once, quickly, a lyrical vision fills the void. A Beatrice or a Blessed Damozel or a Madeleine (Abse, the modest urban understater, just calls her 'a very, *very* pretty girl') leans out of a train-window—*et voilà*, we're just as much back in Provence as at the end of Thomas's poem! Of course, the psychological twist is sharper here: the sense of lost choices (not so much because of the girl's inaccessibility at just this moment as because of the poet's 'much married' state and the whole existential surround of that state) but also the relief at the unreality of the challenge in the two protagonists, now 'daring and secure,' as they wave goodbye to one another. Humor, complacency, philosophizing—all come to soften the blow of defeat on the fields of glamour and free choice. The phrase 'atrocious speed' at the end of the penultimate line is full of displaced dismay. Although the very place-names with which the poem concludes recall the end of Stephen Spender's 'The Express' as well as of 'Adlestrop,' the tone is different—the wry surrender of a vision and a thrilling music.

Despite a certain burdened heaviness and evanescent melancholy in this evoked parting of two non-lovers who never met, 'Not Adlestrop' is cheerful enough in much the same volatile way that 'Adlestrop' is: wry, realistic, full of winning dreams, yet elegiac. To exhibit *some* sort of human morale within the elegiac mode is, precisely, one of the great pressures on modern poetry; a combined vivacity, intensity, and forthrightness is the natural response to that pressure, and in his deployment of these resources Abse again resembles Thomas and other poets of the Great War. His 'Pathology of Colours' is a sharp reminder of the way Wilfred Owen and Siegfried Sassoon (in the remarkable poem 'Repression of War Experience') dealt with the unbearable. Here Abse writes out of medical experience of horror just as they did out of the trenches, without squeamishness and with a blessed, unrhetorical seriousness:

> *I know the colour rose, and it is lovely,*
> *but not when it ripens in a tumour;*
> *and healing greens, leaves and grass, so springlike,*
> *in limbs that fester are not springlike.*
>
> *I have seen red-blue tinged with hirsute mauve*
> *in the plum-skin face of a suicide.*
> *I have seen white, china white almost, stare*
> *from behind the smashed windscreen of a car.*
>
> *And the criminal, multi-coloured flash*
> *of an H-bomb is no more beautiful*
> *than an autopsy when the belly's opened—*
> *to show cathedral windows never opened.*
>
> *So in the simple blessing of a rainbow,*
> *in the bevelled edge of a sunlit mirror,*
> *I have seen, visible, Death's artifact*
> *like a soldier's ribbon on a tunic tacked.*

This poem recalls the wrenched, awkward power of Owen's 'Greater Love'—its impossible insistence on the greater, more exquisite and passionate feeling evoked by the battlefield dead than by the beauty of a loved woman. And the closing stanza goes further (as Sassoon's 'Repression of War Experience' does) in suggesting how lovely or innocuous sights may evoke hideous associations—a reversal of our unwilling recognition of the distortions of beauty lurking in diseased and dead bodies. (The inescapable war-associations in our modern memories make themselves felt in the closing stanzas.) Perhaps Abse's most striking poem of those that cope directly with depressive knowledge in the elegiac mode, however, is the riddling 'Hunt the Thimble'. Here, in the guise of the children's game named in the title, a dialogue takes place in which one supposed speaker questions another about 'it'—some ultimate source of fear and misery—and is constantly put off as the questions grow more and more suggestive of dreariness. ('Is it like heavy rain falling,' or like 'the brooding darkness' inside a provincial Spanish cathedral, or 'like those old men in hospital dying' who 'shout out, "Mama," ' or like 'the darkness inside a dead man's mouth'?)

43

'Hunt the Thimble' may well be Abse's purest poem, with an original turn in its subtly protective tone but nevertheless cumulatively dread-filled dynamics—a method reminiscent of Kenneth Fearing's but without the tough-guy New York rasp of that marvelous, neglected poet. In fact, it is remarkable how often Abse's work makes one think of the best work of other modern poets, not because of any mere derivativeness but because he speaks out of a world and a psyche and a complex of historical memory and anticipation that we recognize and share. His family poems, again, have that combination of idiosyncratic sensibility and a familiar realm of awareness that marks all his writing. They strike the confessional note again and again, but without hysteria or exhibitionism. The quiet poem 'A Night Out' could hardly be more understated, and yet it gets at the heart of everything that gives such an ironic tinge to ordinary life these days—that is, the unavoidable pursuit of our daily needs and pleasures despite the dreadful knowledge of extreme suffering imposed on us at every turn. The poem is a simple anecdote. The poet and his wife have gone to see 'the new Polish film' recommended by friends, an almost-documentary film about Auschwitz: 'the human obscenity in close-up.' The atmosphere of the 'ever melancholy queue / of cinemas', and then of the theatre itself, and then of the Camp scenes (including an inner irony of the Camp orchestra performing 'the solemn gaiety of Bach'), and of the confusions of real and unreal—'those striped victims merely actors'—in the passive receptivity of the audience is unfolded quietly but indelibly:

> *We watched, as we munched milk chocolate,*
> *trustful children, no older than our own,*
> *strolling into the chambers without fuss,*
> *while smoke, black and curly, oozed from chimneys.*

And then? The couple leave the theatre, have coffee 'in a bored espresso bar nearby,' drive home, and

> *We asked the au pair girl from Germany*
> *if anyone had phoned at all, or called,*
> *and, of course, if the children had woken.*
> *Reassured, together we climbed the stairs,*
> *undressed together, and naked together,*
> *in the dark, in the marital bed, made love.*

It's the plain helplessness about what to do with one's awareness, not only of the stench of continuing history but of all the ironies noted in so many details of the poem, that leaves such a coppery taste in one's mouth. The sense of being merely actors ourselves in some sort of irreversibly progressing film makes the sexual act at the end an embodiment of the elegiac, a possible contribution to the Auschwitz of the future, and a betrayal of grief. None of these thoughts are advanced by the poem itself; there is no lugubrious pontificating such as we might find in Auden or Larkin. The little anecdote about what is, after all, a common enough sort of experience presents itself and stops. Not that it lacks indicative language concerning its range of awareness; no, the whole of that range is part of the anecdote, and it includes all the depths of self-reproach at 'living as usual' that constitute the abyss above which we hover in our time. But it also provides, with sufficient organic density, an atmosphere of normal human experience such as neither Auden nor Larkin, despite their considerable talents, provides.

In the same way, while Auden, say, is 'European' by virtue of his reading and political interests, Abse is 'European' without half trying, because he is so intimately Jewish without religious parochialism or defensiveness. Thus, the first stanzas of 'Uncle Isidore':

> *When I observe a toothless ex-violinist,*
> *with more hair than face, sprawled like Karl Marx*
> *on a park seat or slumped, dead or asleep,*
> *in the central heat of a public library*
> *I think of Uncle Isidore—smelly*
> *schnorrer and lemon-tea bolshevik—my foreign*
> *distant relative, not always distant.*
>
> *Before Auschwitz, Treblinka, he seemed near,*
> *those days of local pogroms, five-year programmes,*
> *until I heard him say, 'Master, Master*
> *of the Universe, blessed be your name,*
> *don't you know there's been no rain for years*
> *and your people are thirsty? Have you no shame,*
> *compassion? Don't you care at all?'*

And in the touching portrait of his dying father's courage and indifference to suffering called 'In Llandough Hospital,' Abse gives us a simile out of the heart of modern Europe such as neither Larkin nor Auden would have conceived: 'He's thin as Auschwitz in that bed.' This is a natural image for a modern Jewish sensibility, at once internationalist, politically conscious, and, as it were, continuously in mourning whatever the context (even when it is boisterously comic, as in a few of the lines I have been quoting). It seems to me that this historically elegiac dimension enters even the least politically colored poems, such as 'In the Theatre,' that Abse has written. 'In the Theatre' (subtitled '*A True Incident*') describes an operation in which the surgeon destroys a patient's brain as he probes (the date is 1938, before more precise methods had been developed) for a brain tumor.

> *Lambert Rogers desperate, fingering still;*
> *his dresser thinking, 'Christ! Two more on the list,*
> *a cisternal puncture and a neural cyst.'*
>
> *Then, suddenly, the cracked record in the brain,*
> *a ventriloquist voice that cried, 'You sod,*
> *leave my soul alone, leave my soul alone,'—*
> *the patient's dummy lips moving to that refrain,*
> *the patient's eyes too wide. And, shocked,*
> *Lambert Rogers drawing out the probe*
> *with nurses, students, sister, petrified.*

Abse doesn't even look for reassurance in his poems; and yet the morale remains—an energizing if thoroughly unpretentious sense of human coping, if only through sensitively accurate perception of things as they are and prevailing good will that is warm and humorous whenever given half a chance. Of all the current English poets, he is the one who tries least to impress us—whether with athletic energies, or withering (and self-withering) wit, or scholarship in the service of nostalgia or local pride. More than the others, though, he speaks for our day and for the way we are moving through it. Without having any such thought in mind, doubtless, he is our gentlest existentialist.

Way Out in the Centre

DANIEL HOFFMAN

The title of Dannie Abse's latest book, *Way Out in the Centre*, is self-descriptive, the poet's placing of his own work in relation to both the tradition of English poetry and the counter-tradition of Modernism. The titular phrase occurs in his poem, 'A note to Donald Davie in Tennessee,' so I take it that Abse is defining his position, at least in part, in the context of Donald Davie's adjurations to British poets that they take Basil Bunting, George Oppen, and Louis Zukofsky as their models. These poets work from 'the conviction that a poem is a transaction between the poet and his subject more than it is a transaction between the poet and his readers.' Davie's proposing that the Objectivist method, and particularly the work of Bunting, points to 'where English poetry has got to, and where it may go next (at our hands, if we so choose),' is offered in his essay, 'English and American in *Briggflats*,' which Dannie Abse reprinted in his annual anthology, *Best of the Poetry Year 6* (London: Robson Books, 1979). In 'A note to Donald Davie in Tennessee,' Abse replies to his friend's polemic in a tone characteristically understated, saying, 'Still poets / jog eagerly, each molehill mistaken / for Parnassus,' and, he asks, 'where's the avant-garde when the procession / runs continuously in a closed circle?' Abse concludes with lines that reward our scrutiny:

> *I too am a reluctant puritan, feel uneasy*
> *sometimes as if I travelled without ticket,*
> *Yet here I am in England way out in the centre.*

47

On reflection one must ask, if 'in the centre,' why 'way out' and travelling 'without ticket'? Abse's titular phrase is an oxymoron the contradictions of which extend to the poem it describes. I propose to identify several characteristic themes in Abse's work and, exploring these in one or two poems devoted to each, suggest how this poet is both 'In England' and 'in the centre,' yet 'way out,' travelling 'without ticket.'

Since the Second World War English poetry has been dominated, in turn, by the domestic muse, the scaled-down sense of possibilities, of the Movement and the Group poets; by the vehement rejection of such limitations in the violent primitivism of Ted Hughes; and by the meditative mythopoetics of Geoffrey Hill. The genuineness of Abse's work depends on neither the ironic use of traditional forms and meters, as with Larkin; nor on the wrenching disjunctions of syntax or leaps of associative imagery, as with Hughes; nor in the allusive, chthonic probings of Hill. Nor, as may be inferred, does Abse resemble Charles Tomlinson, who more than any of his English contemporaries anticipated Davie's advice and sought models in American modernism. If these poets are indisputably and typically English, then Abse's work is triangulated not near any of the extreme positions each has taken but at a distance from all of them, way out in the centre.

Abse's aim, as he says in his preface to *Collected Poems*, is 'to write poems which appear translucent but are in fact deceptions. I would have a reader enter them, be deceived he could see through them like sea-water, and be puzzled when he can not quite touch bottom.' Or, as he writes in a late poem, 'The Test,'

> *Oh the irreducible strangeness of things*
> *and the random purposes of dreams.*

Or, as in 'Mysteries,'

> *I should know by now that few octaves can be heard,*
> *that a vision dies from being too long stared at;*
> . . . .
> *. . . . I start with the visible*
> *and am startled by the visible.*

If such lines indicate a concentration upon perception, others explore the mystery of the perceiver's identity:

48

Not for one second, I know,
can I be the same man twice.
('Leaving Cardiff')

my two voices sing to make one rhyme
('Duality')

These quotations introduce several terms recurrent in Abse's work: strangeness, things, dreams, purposes, vision, the visible, and the sense of duality whenever the speaker's identity is defined.

Abse is a skeptical humanist, desiring belief by relying upon the visible—which in turn rewards him with moments 'when small mirrors of reality blaze / into miracles.' Yet in another poem, one entitled 'Miracles,' a priest says to him,

> *A doctor must believe*
> *in miracles, but I, a priest, dare not.*
>
> *Then my incurable cancer patient,*
> *the priest, sat up in bed, looked to the window,*
> *and peeled his tangerine, silently.*

The conversational tone is maintained with such calm and verisimilitude that language and rhetoric seem to do little to heighten tension; yet the meaning, the doubleness of implication, rises, all but imperceptibly, in the reader's awareness. That the doctor must have faith while the priest dares not is a reflexive proposition, since 'faith,' in this context, must refer to both assurance of God and hope of being cured. Yet how sever these from one another?

Like the lapsed Christian bicyclist in Larkin's 'Church-Going,' Abse is unable to participate in his inherited faith (or any other—see 'Even'), though for him—and this is one of the markers of the distance his central position is way out from those of the other English poets of his generation—the faith in which he cannot believe is not the Church of England, or even chapel, but Judaism. Another marker is the distance, psychological as well as linear, between Cardiff and London, for Dannie Abse is not only Jewish but Welsh. Yet again, as he writes in 'Odd,' he is always the odd man out: when at home in his respectable suburb, 'by the neighbours am considered odd'; but when 'From the sensible wastes of Golders Green / I journey to Soho where a job owns me,' in that 'not . . . respectable place' he is once again 'considered odd.' Not only because divided between bourgeois householder and bohemian poet, but also because the job that 'owns' him is that of medical practitioner. The deeper division is between the scientific objectivity of the physician and the sensibility—introspective, humane—of the poet. Of course the poet's job—which also 'owns' him—is to use both sides of each of these divisions—British/Jewish, English/Welsh, seeker/skeptic, bourgeois/bohemian, poet/doctor—in the poems.

The dichotomies between doctor/poet and skeptic/seeker are dramatized perhaps most memorably in Abse's poem 'In the Theatre.' The theatre is the operating room, in a teaching hospital, of a brain surgeon over forty years ago (the poem is based on an operation witnessed by the poet's brother, Dr. Wilfred Abse), when the only way to locate a brain tumor was to open the skull and feel for it. The patient is under local anaesthetic and conscious, the physician's fingers, 'rash as a blind man's,' probing, probing, 'the growth / still undiscovered, ticking its own wild time,' until

> . . . suddenly, the cracked record in the brain,
> a ventriloquist voice that cried, 'You sod,
> leave my soul alone, leave my soul alone,'—
> the patient's dummy lips moving to that refrain,
> the patient's eyes too wide.

Then, as the shocked surgeon withdraws the probe, 'that voice so arctic and that cry so odd . . . wound down' like an 'antique gramophone,'

> To cease at last when something other died.
> And silence matched the silence under snow.

Compassion is everywhere evident in Abse's work, as is the way the language without strain introduces metaphors riven with implication. While 'In the Theatre' would seem to affirm the reality of the soul, the patient speaks in 'a ventriloquist voice' which, as he is dying, 'wound down' like an 'antique gramophone.' These tropes maintain to the end—to the end of life, at any rate—that the body is but a mechanism controlled by physical forces.

In 'The Water Diviner' Abse had explored the symbiosis of faith and doubt: 'Late, I have come to a parched land / doubting my gift, if gift I have. . .'

> *The sun flies on*
> *arid wastes, barren hells too warm,*
> *and me with a hazel stick!*
> *. . . .*
>
> *sometimes hearing water trickle,*
> *sometimes not, I, by doubting first,*
> *believe; believing, doubt.*

In 'The Magician,' Abse deals with another figure who possesses, or thinks or pretends he possesses, extraordinary power. The stage magician in the poem is a trope for the artist or poet:

> *Sometimes, something he cannot understand*
> *happens—atavistic powers stray unleashed,*
> *a raving voice he hardly thought to hear,*
> *the ventriloquist's dummy out of hand.*

Here the ventriloquist is the artist-figure, whose dummy may take on a life of its own: an implication which reflects on the use of the same metaphor in the poem about the botched brain surgery. The mysterious 'atavistic power' which the magician 'cannot understand' is dramatized compellingly in Abse's recent play, *Pythagoras* (1979). There, as in 'The Magician,' the very existence of such power is both affirmed and doubted; yet we tend to come away from play and poem persuaded that something real has been put before us, whether the poet or reader can define it or not.

The very title of Abse's *Poems: Golders Green* (1961) is another oxymoron, since the two halves seem mutually exclusive. This dichotomy is explored in the poem 'Odd,' discussed above, and in others in this and his subsequent collections. The title of this book introduces into Abse's work poems concerning his identity as a Jew. The theme is approached in 'After the release of Ezra Pound,' in which the complexity of Pound's case is acknowledged, as is the difficulty of forgiving him. In 'Red Balloon' Abse explores the source of prejudice in a ballad-like fable about himself as a boy in Cardiff—

51

> 'It's a Jew's balloon,' my best friend cried,
> 'stained with our dear Lord's blood,'
>
> . . . .
>
> 'Your red balloon's a Jew's balloon,
> let's get it circumcised.'
>
> Then some boys laughed and some boys cursed,
> some unsheathed their dirty knives;
> some lunged, some clawed at my balloon,
> but still it would not burst.

The oddness of the story and the simplicity of the ballad structure make the 'Red Balloon' memorable, all the more so for its evocation of perhaps the oldest literary expression in English poetry of persecution of the Jews. Abse's red balloon surely suggests the ball thrown by Sir Hugh into the Jew's window in 'Sir Hugh, or the Jew's Daughter' (Child 155); that ballad accuses the Jews of ritual murder of the boy (the same motif used by Chaucer's Prioress). Abse's reversal of the story's implications is all the stronger for his allusions to medieval precedents. The lad in his poem is experiencing the history of the Jews.

The theme of Jewish identity recurs in such later poems as 'A Night Out' and 'No more Mozart.' In the first of these the poet and his wife see a Polish film about Auschwitz—'We watched, as we munched milk chocolate, / trustful children, no older than our own, / strolling into the chambers without fuss. . .' It is hard to make the imaged reality a part of one's own life. But in 'No More Mozart,' written after a first visit to Germany.

> The German streets tonight
> are soaped in moonlight.
> The streets of Germany are clean
> like the hands of Lady Macbeth.
>
> . . . .
>
> Now, of course, no more Mozart.
> With eyes closed still
> the body touches itself, takes stock.
> Above the hands the thin wrists
> attached to them; and on the wrists
> the lampshade material. . .

Now, the speaker sees as did 'twelve million eyes / in six million heads.'

In *Funland* (1972), the new poems in *Collected Poems* (1977), and in *Way Out in the Centre* (1981) the poem with Jewish themes are for the most part either sketches of family members or retellings of Talmudic wisdom literature in which rabbis stand on one leg while delivering *mots justes*. These latter, such as 'Tales of Shatz,' 'Rabbi Yose,' and 'Snake' have the charm of folktales. Perhaps it is with this part of his identity in mind that Abse describes his own journey as one in which he 'feel[s] / uneasy / sometimes as if I travelled without ticket. / Yet here I am in England. . . .'

If the central English tradition since Wordsworth has been concerned with the poet's relationship to nature, then Abse is decidedly 'way out.' He has written his *ars poetica* explicitly in several poems besides 'A note to Donald Davie' (who, far off in 'fugitive' territory, Tennessee, would tell English poets the rules of their art). One of these is 'Not Adlestrop.' Again the title is a key, this one referring to Edward Thomas's poem, 'Adlestrop,' which we may take as at the centre of the Georgian tradition. Thomas made a pastoral idyll of a moment at a deserted railway depot; but Abse's moment in such a place is *not* 'Adlestrop'; instead of experiencing among the works of industrial man an epiphany in the presence of songbirds, Abse exchanges a momentary glimpse, from the platform, with a pretty girl on a departing train. Abse's tone is always conversational, for his is a poetry which assumes the presence of a reader to whom the poet's feelings and illuminations are being communicated. Thus the objectivism of Bunting and Oppen, which Davie rightly locates in their alienation from their audience, is as foreign to Abse's purpose as is their tone to his style. In style and purpose, in its relation to its reader, Abse's poem *is* in the mainstream of English verse, though, writing in mid-twentieth century, Abse locates feeling in relation to social experience rather than in his response to the natural world. 'I'll not compete with those nature poets you advance' he tells a woman who questions his seriousness for not doing so ('As I was saying'); 'Urban, I should mug up anew' in a book from W. H. Smith the once-evocative names of wild flowers.

As an urban poet, Abse has responded to the London he lives in, and poems of his, with a quiet eloquence as convincing as the work of any of the Movement poets of the 1950s and '60s, limn the sense of dwindled possibilities which afflicted England in the years after

53

the Second World War. In such poems as 'Public Library' and 'The Shunters' Abse writes of 'bed-sitting rooms,' 'rainy, dejected railway stations,' 'the colour of grief . . . In the tired afternoon drizzle,' 'a despair beyond language.' At that time, however, Abse had taken a polemical position opposing that of the Movement—or rather, a position opposing the polemics of the Movement, which excluded from a foothill of Parnassus all poets not of like mind with Robert Conquest (*New Lines*, 1956). Abse, together with Howard Sergeant, in 1957 published a rival anthology entitled *Mavericks*, offered, as young poets 'writing from the centre of inner experience,' David Wright, Vernon Scannell, Michael Hamburger, Jon Silkin, several others, and Abse himself. There was doubtless too much smoke and fire on both sides of this controversy, which in some quarters generated ill-will that lasted for years. In fact the Movement proved not really a movement, its poets sharing little besides a general attitude; and the Mavericks also each went their separate ways. The ironic trope in Abse's title *Poems: Golders Green* and the implied reduction of 'primary Dionysian excitement' in his next title, *A Small Desperation*, show him determined to mine his own life, however prosaic its surface reality, for poems 'from the centre of inner experience.'

Characteristically, Abse sees himself not alone in a field of flowers but in relation to others. Growing up in the working class, in Wales, where his elder brother Leo became a prominent Labor M.P., it is not surprising that this poet should have founded a magazine entitled *Poetry and Poverty*, or be concerned with political themes. He has said that it was the reading of Spanish Republican poets like Miguel Hernandez in his youth that opened the possibilities of poetry to him. Yet his outright political poems on specific issues are few, and no more successful than the polemics of others. Abse acknowledges that such direct treatment accomplishes little:

> *Righteous the rhetoric of indignation,*
> *but protesting poems, like the plaster angels,*
> *are impotent. They commit no crimes,*
> *they pass no laws; they grant amnesty*
> *only to those who, in safety, write them.*
> ('Remembering Miguel Hernandez')

When Abse's political concerns are merged with his larger humane and liberal sympathies and are expressed in fables, his

54

poems have an amplitude of meaning and an inexorability which makes them memorable. His 'Emperors of the Island' (in *Tenants of the House*, 1956), subtitled 'A Political Parable To Be Read Aloud,' has the lilting structure of an incremental nursery rhyme, and the grim determinism of a prophecy.

In 'Funland,' the long title poem of his 1972 volume, Abse's political concerns merge with his distrust of scientific rationalism as the basis for the organization of society. Here the governing metaphor is familiar enough; a madhouse is a world. What is original in Abse's treatment is the way that what begins as a comic turn, becomes more ominous as it becomes more mad and more extensive, so that by the end of his nine-part poem the metaphor is reversed and we have a whole world gone mad. At the same time his inmates—the superintendent, an atheist uncle, Fat Blondie, the poet, and Pythagoras (who 'wanted to found / a Society not a Religion'—and did so by inventing Thracians, a people who could be excluded)—all these are so individualized that although we know them to be mad, we cannot withhold our sympathies from them. Pythagoras seizes power when the superintendent dies—all are deathly afraid of death.

> *Let Pythagoras be*
> *an example to all Thracian spies*
> *my tyrant uncle cried*

as 'Funland' suddenly and starkly becomes a political fable. It immediately modulates into something more universal:

> *Who's next for the icepick?*
>
> *Already the severed head of Pythagoras*
> *transforms the flagpole*
> *into a singularly*
> *long white neck.*
>
> *It has become a god that cannot see*
> *how the sun drips its dilutions*
> *on dumpy snowacres.*

Abse has boldly invaded the territory of the satirical novel of the absurd, as though intensifying what Orwell, Golding, or Burgess might have written out in several hundred pages. The transformation of the games of Funland into political conspiracy and murder into tribal ritual is as compelling as the stark rhythms and images in which they are presented. The movement is fragmented, disrupted, while the air echoes with unexpressed implications. Abse himself felt this, for the figure of Pythagoras, invented for 'Funland,' arrogated to himself a larger structure in a different form. In 1976 Abse's play, *Pythagoras*, was produced by the Birmingham Repertory Theatre and was published in 1979. Here the setting is still a lunatic asylum, with a couple of doctors representing scientism and official order, while the patients may well stand for the rest of mankind. Among them is Pythagoras, who before incarceration was a stage magician (as in Abse's poem 'The Magician'), and who believes himself the reincarnation of the Greek philosopher whose name he has taken. He is a touching and compelling figure of irrationality, the irreducible individuality, the spiritual independence and imaginative power of the human being. The play is a comic, ironical, and memorable fable in which political implications are subsumed in considerations of order *vs.* freedom, rationalism *vs.* belief, identity *vs.* appearance, the claims of science to understand everything *vs.* the imagination with its mysterious secrets. In short, the characteristic complex of themes in Abse's poems.

Abse's poems are indeed at once 'in the centre' of the English tradition, yet 'way out' from the terrain marked out by prominent contemporaries. Feeling himself a man speaking to other men and women, though sometimes 'uneasy,' he has been no more tempted than have most other English poets by the modernist sensibility with its isolation from an audience, its radical rejections of conventional rhetoric and its formal innovations. Working from within established traditions, Abse has enlarged the subjects and the range of feelings which he uses these to express. His rhythms are accentual-syllabic, creating the illusion of a conversational voice, a muted music, a continuity of discourse. His tone is quite his own, attractively enticing the reader into the poem before the reader knows where he has been brought, what realizations he must come to. We meet, we watch, we listen, as to his 'Three Street Musicians' who sing and play old tunes,

> And, *as breadcrumbs thrown*
> *on the ground charm sparrows down from nowhere,*
> *now, suddenly, there are too many ghosts about.*

Poet of an Uncommon Reality

JEREMY HOOKER

In 'Duality,' a poem of the early nineteen fifties, Dannie Abse
describes himself as a man with 'two voices' singing 'to make one
rhyme.' If this were only an isolated statement it would prove
nothing—the stance of the poet as a person inwardly divided and at
odds with society is a cliché of imitative poets, who borrow it from
the Romantics or the moderns to express a vague unease, or to cut a
poetic figure. On the other hand, duality is a fact of the Romantic
movement, and a fact of modern poetry in the Romantic tradition,
which bears the strain of tension between dream and reality, art and
life, prophecy and introspection, or cracks under it. It was a fact for
Wilfred Owen and Alun Lewis, for example, and it is a fact in their
poetry. For that is where the crucial difference between duality as a
secondhand theme and lived duality shows itself, in the conflicts
helping to make or break the poem. In Lewis's case, the duality of
love and death was embodied in the metaphor of a frontier. The
metaphor dramatised his personal predicament, but was developed
from the work of W. H. Auden and his fellow social poets of the
thirties. In fact, a frontier or border is common ground for many
modern poets in Britain, and although the metaphor is open to
many different uses, it generally reflects the poet's ambiguous relation to society. I want in this essay to show that a lived duality is
present as a shaping factor in Dannie Abse's work, and that his
poetry exists in the tension between opposing impulses, and sometimes in their reconciliation.

'Duality' itself is not a particularly convincing poem. It has the sort of symbolical-cum-allegorical structure that Dannie Abse has largely abandoned in his later development. For this reason, it names in general terms tensions that are usually more specific in his maturer work:

> Death I love and Death I hate,
> (I'll be with you soon and late).
> Love I love and Love I loathe,
> God I mock and God I prove,
> yes, myself I kill, myself I save.

Here, the great themes remain abstract; in his later poems, ambivalent feelings about death, love, God and the self are usually rooted in particular experiences.

The main causes of Dannie Abse's duality are obvious, and he has reflected on them in *A Poet in the Family*, as well as dramatized them in his poetry. He is a poet and a doctor. He is a Welsh Jew. It will be useful here to state some of the implications of these facts, as shown in his autobiography and poems, or inferred from them.

Dannie Abse trained as a scientist, and grew up with a strong social conscience, but began to develop as a poet in the quasi-Romantic literary climate of the forties, when Dylan Thomas and the social, clinical Auden of the previous decade were powerful, opposing influences. As a doctor, he has daily experience of human suffering, and is what he calls, in 'The Test,' 'licensed friend to Caliban.' He is also a well-known literary figure, moving in a world which, on the whole, prefers to leave actual Calibans unbefriended; and in any case, he knows the limits of practical help for physical or mental suffering, and the culpability of general affirmations that cloud the many particular instances of torment in a rhetoric of universal good. He is 'a fortunate man,' capable of expressing great happiness in love; but, moving uneasily between Cardiff and London, or Golders Green and Soho, he is not completely at home anywhere. He is highly aware of the prophetic role of the poet, emphasised by the Hebrew and the Welsh literary traditions, as well as by the ideas of 'commitment' which have been influential in England in his lifetime. He is a nonconformist, a maverick, 'a Daniel condemned/to prove timeless honesties' ('New Babylons'). But he is also one threatened by the 'they' of 'Social revolution in England.' He is, therefore, like Auden and Lewis, inwardly divided between prophet and victim, and if on occasions he can sound remarkably like Lewis at his most Audenesque, this is partly because the internal and external fronts at which he finds himself in peacetime have much in common with the soldier-poet's:

> . . . *from this shore of cold I write*
> *tiny flashes in the night.*
>
> . . . .
>
> *Dear, vague as a distant star, I,*
> *in the huge night's amorphous lie,*
> *find one small and luminous truth*
> *of which our usual love was proof.*
>
> ('Poem and message')

In *A Poet in the Family* Dannie Abse records his response, in 1940, to poems by Miguel Hernandez in *Poems for Spain*: 'Here was a voice that could arouse a reader's indignation and, perhaps, *move him to action*. Here was a persuasive, pleading, prophetic and admonitory voice and one, which, in some unspecified future I hoped to emulate.' In 'Remembering Miguel Hernandez,' a poem of the nineteen sixties, he expresses a different view:

> *Righteous the rhetoric of indignation,*
> *but protesting poems, like the plaster angels,*
> *are impotent. They commit no crimes,*
> *they pass no laws; they grant amnesty*
> *only to those who, in safety, write them.*

His autobiography tells the story of his growth from young, would-be prophet to a man with a much more complex understanding of his position and the nature and demands of his poetic gift. But although Dannie Abse has come to admire quieter voices and subtler realisms, notably Edward Thomas's and William Carlos Williams', his sense of urgency has increased with his heightened consciousness of being a Jew, through taking in 'more fully the unbearable reality of what happened in Europe,' and he remains a poet seeking a public voice. On the last page of *A Poet in the Family*, published in 1974, he says: 'Writing poetry, too, was an immersion into common reality not an escape from it.'

59

Dannie Abse has written a number of moving poems about 'common reality,' in which he has found a public voice. He is a public man in his roles as doctor and poet, and of the poems arising from these roles those deriving from the former ('The smile was' and 'Pathology of colours,' for example) are more impressive and affecting in their attention to their subject than the more self-conscious poems, such as 'Florida' and 'As I was saying,' deriving from the latter. He can tell a story movingly in verse, as in 'Cousin Sidney.' There is no question of his compassion or concern, or of his ability to amuse or disturb. But it is not as a poet immersed in common reality that he is most original, although even as such a poet, his duality makes him a realist in his images and descriptions of the facts of suffering and death, but obviates the exclusion of mystery.

Indeed, the earliest poem Dannie Abse includes in *Collected Poems 1948–1976*, 'The uninvited,' is a poem of strange visitation, in which 'they,' in their 'unasked for' coming into and leaving 'our lives,' have brought 'the weight of another world.' It is the poem of a haunted man, open to a troubling mystery.

The romanticism of Dannie Abse may be seen in his daring and colourful metaphors and images, his surrealistic effects and biblical symbols. These are present early and late, but with differences.

'Epithalamion' is original, early Abse, but also very much a poem of the forties. Its repeated variations on 'all the living and all the dead' recall Dylan Thomas and Vernon Watkins, and its imagery is reminiscent of Alun Lewis's in his most romantic love poems. But its ecstatic tone and the exhilaration that breaks out in a sudden splash of verbal colour are original:

> Shipwrecked, the sun sinks down harbours
> of a sky, unloads its liquid cargoes
> of marigolds, and I and my white girl
> lie still in the barley . . .

Only compare this, from a well-known, early Abse poem, with the colours of a much later, probably more famous poem:

> I know the colour rose, and it is lovely,
> but not when it ripens in a tumour;
> and healing greens, leaves and grass, so springlike,
> in limbs that fester are not springlike.

I have seen red-blue tinged with hirsute mauve
in the plum-skin face of a suicide.
I have seen white, china white almost, stare
from behind the smashed windscreen of a car.

('Pathology of colours')

'Pathology of Colours' voices the suspicion of nature used as an escape from harsh human and natural realities that is a recurrent theme of Dannie Abse's poetry. It may also be an ironical comment on Vernon Watkins's 'Music of Colours' sequence, but it is surely a sardonic reflection on the poetic permissiveness of the forties, which allowed a riot of metaphor, a verbal inflation and a vague affirmative symbolism, in which particular realities were lost, and in which the realist Abse's meanings were sometimes obscured by the romantic Abse's colourful poetic figures.

But of course, realism and romanticism are not necessarily at odds. On the contrary, the original Romantic movement sought a new realism, cleansing the vision of common reality and expanding imaginative sympathy to embrace it. Much later, the Wilfred Owen who went to war with a Keatsian dream world in his head, found in Keats the support of compassionate realism. Interestingly, 'Pathology of colours' uses a technique similar to Owen's opposition of Romantic realism to romantic dream, as when, for example, he compares the redness of girls' lips with the red stones 'kissed' by soldiers' blood. In Owen's wartime poems the soldier answers the young poet, but in the same Romantic terms, which he now understands. Similarly, in 'Pathology of colours' the doctor answers the young poet in a language common to both, but used with a difference. The similarity is made more marked by the fact that the poet-doctor sees 'in the simple blessing of a rainbow,' 'Death's artifact/like a soldier's ribbon on a tunic tacked.' This is still the same poet who, like Alex Comfort, in the verse letter Abse addressed to him, 'dug deep/into the wriggling earth for a rainbow with an honest spade.'

Romantic poetry also has a prophetic voice and an introspective voice, which may sing as one, but with great difficulty. Dannie Abse's work reveals how he has repeatedly faced the problem of writing in a public manner when the man is moved by public issues and large themes but the poet, though drawn to them by compassion, conscience and poetic ambition, is at his best when most intimate, and when shaping a vision of things that are not commonly seen and felt. For he is most memorable when least explicit and most oblique, and when appearing to speak either to himself or intimately to another.

An imaginative centre which attracts these qualities is what one poem calls 'the nameless things,/or rather the unnameable.' This is present in poems evoking the atmosphere of desolate urban places, which often use it to intimate mortality or the spirit of disregarded people or things, or a dimension beyond consciousness. These include 'The shunters,' 'From a suburban window,' 'Halls' and 'Olfactory pursuits.'

In two lines of 'The shunters,' describing trains running out of sight—

> *In the tired afternoon drizzle, their smoke*
> *fades into industrial England.*

he begins with the visible and moves off into distances which are strangely more than geographical and temporal, enacting the process that produces some of his most haunting effects. This passage is immediately preceded by an Audenesque line ('Only posh expresses sport proper names') which is alien to the spirit of the poem, for it is a social comment, close in manner to Auden's discursiveness, that does not belong with the intimations of this poetic world. 'After a departure' is also marked by Auden's influence but is like 'The shunters' in reflecting Abse's special way of seeing and feeling common things uncommonly:

> *Intimate god of stations,*
> *on long, faded afternoons*
> *before impatient trains depart,*
> *where the aching lovers wait*
> *and mothers embarrass sons,*
> *discover your natural art;*
> *delicately articulate*
> *an elegy of the heart*
> *for horizons appropriate . . .*

It may be that this is Dannie Abse's natural art too, and that if he always articulated elegies of the heart he would be a consistently haunting poet. But he would be a less ambitious and daring poet as well.

'Olfactory pursuits' is one of his most original and memorable poems. Here too the poet begins with the particular, an oddly unsettling sensuous action:

Often, unobserved, I smell my own hand.

and at once sets off in search of 'something forgotten,' like Edward Thomas following the scent of the herb in 'Old Man.' At the heart of the poem the poet exclaims:

> *Christ, what is it I'm after?*
>
> *I dream, without sleeping, of things obscure,*
> *of houses and streets and temples deserted*
> *which, if once visited, I don't recall.*

It is not a poem in which the poet is wiser than his poem, asking questions he knows the answer to, and using it to conceal or disclose pre-existing knowledge. Nor should the reader claim a wisdom the poet does not have, by answering the question for him. Rather, as in 'Old Man,' he shares the mysterious experience with the poet, and is led into obscure places of his own, perhaps common to all:

> *My footfall echoes down old foundations,*
> *buried mosaics, tomb tablets crumbled,*
> *flints in the grass, your ruins or my ruins.*
>
> *A man sniffs the back of his own hand,*
> *moistens it with his mouth, to sniff again,*
> *to think a blank; writes, 'The odour of stones.'*

Or if not common to all, memories in the deep well of the human mind, then common to those who share the peculiarly modern experience of existing precariously on shifting ground between past and present, between common reality and a more mysterious world, between the conviction that present life in the flesh is all there is, and the haunting sense that time is not what it seems.

The religious impulse in 'Olfactory pursuits' surfaces with surprising explicitness in 'Christ, what is it I'm after?' Or does it? For while the abruptness of the exclamation makes it sound like a cry, it is also just possible that the emotion giving rise to it is impatience,

63

and 'Christ' a mere expletive. This is characteristic, for although the religious impulse in Dannie Abse's poetry is strong, it is usually countered by irony. His duality in this respect is nearly captured in the following lines from 'The grand view':

> I do not know who
> is is that I love, but I would flow
> into One invisible and still.
>
> Though islanded and inspired by
> the merely human, I . . .

In this poem, and elsewhere, there is stalemate between desire for a transcendent unity and a strong humanism, which produces a tone of Prufrockian indecisiveness:

> My forehead is open. The horns grow out
> and exit. Infirm cynics knock inside,
> and still ancestral voices shout
> visions, visions! Should I turn about
> if, by naming all, One is denied?

Yet this tortuous doubting self-consciousness coexists in the poem with the directness of

> There are moments when a man must sing
> of a lone Presence he cannot see.

Dannie Abse is constantly at war with irony, and constantly draws back from defeating it. On the one hand, it represents the habitual curb on strong feeling and poetic ambition that succeeded the excesses of the forties in English poetry and is still widely in evidence in spite of the appearance of Ted Hughes and 'confessional' poetry. Dannie Abse is no friend to this limiting irony as an end in itself. On the other hand, it serves as humanism that is properly deeply suspicious of the false comfort and essential complacency of a vague and inflated use of emotive or religious terms, and is a necessary defence of the particular against its absorption in a groundless universality. Which is not to say that genuine and even great religious poetry has not been written in Britain since T. S. Eliot's acknowledged achievement, but that it has been written against considerable odds, in a language strewn with decayed symbols. In this situation, the ironist is closer than the blithe symbolist to the true religious poet.

Dannie Abse has undergone, in his own way, the Romantic poet's critical transition from dreams to responsibilities. But happily, just as Yeats never did walk naked, Abse has not taken literally the advice he gave himself in 'The water diviner':

> I should have built, plain brick on brick,
> a water tower.

I say happily, not because such plainness cannot produce great poetry, but because his gifts are not those of the poets for whose writing the building of a brick water tower is a reasonably apt metaphor: William Carlos Williams and George Oppen.

It was a Romantic poet, not an Objectivist, who painted the realistic picture of 'Pathology of colours' with the vividness of 'Epithalamion.' Mature Abse would not universalize his love as he did in that early poem:

> Listen flowers, birds, winds, worlds,
> tell all today that I married
> more than a white girl in the barley—
> for today I took to my human bed
> flower and bird and wind and world,
> and all the living and all the dead.

But neither has he ceased, where possible, to praise, or wonder.

In his Introductory Note to *Collected Poems 1948–1976* Dannie Abse writes of his enduring ambition 'to look upon the world with the eyes of a perpetual convalescent.' An outcome of the ambition may be seen in 'Surprise! Surprise!' where he writes

> Everything is alien, everyone strange.

and

> Oh how everything and everybody
> are perplexed and perplexing, deeply unknown.

Even before the poem begins, its title suggests an ironical half turning away from what it will affirm. The gesture is not uncommon in Dannie Abse's poetry, where the visionary has to listen to his sceptical alter ego, the realist with his refusal of excess, his distrust of large gestures made in the face of the evil and suffering in the world. But if the poet has to hear the scientist in Abse, their duality is by no means always an opposition. For the perpetual convalescent is a Romantic realist. He walks out into the world a little shakily, a familiar of mortality, but gratefully, wondering at being alive, and he sees things as they are, without the full and complacent vision of convention (the view, too often, of common reality), but mysterious, strange, uncommonly real.

Music and Meaning

PETER PORTER

I had known Dannie Abse's poetry for many years before I first met him. I suppose I may have encountered him at some poetry reading in the late fifties or sixties (such things were not so common in those days): certainly he took the chair at a Ben Uri reading I was at, though my memory will not reveal to me whether I was a reader, or only a listener on this occasion. But far more vividly there is my recall of issues of *Poetry and Poverty*, edited, I discovered later, from Belsize Park, the very district where I had gone through my statutory literary despair and exile in 1952/3. One Abse poem from early on haunted me—it seemed to me when I read it first wonderfully witty and arcane. This was (and is) 'Letter to *The Times*.' It still seems these things, but now I hear in it accents, not just of voice but of mind, which are not less moving for being familiar, for constituting a moral presence and an ambience in which art and feeling can move. I think I have heard Dannie Abse read this poem only once.

'The Trial.' I have heard him read much more often. As I look at the page, his voice comes to my mind as clearly as if I had a tape of it: 'Some say high and some say low/to swing, swing, swing, when the free winds blow.' He is, most people would agree, a marvellous reader of his own work. Yet, not especially, a histrionic one. He does not belong to the order of cabaret poets, or to the contrivers of phillipics. He is a secular cantor, rather, though even this misleads if it suggests that he intones his work. It seems to me that he invests it with melody and brings out as 'musical' the ordinary devices of syntax, assonance, dissonance and repetition. No poet writing

67

today, at least since Auden, knows so well how to use a refrain. Abse follows Yeats in believing that poetry is the most musical of the forms of literature. But meaning is to verse what tonality is to music, and Abse's poetry is never just sound, Sitwellian osculation and ululating. His poems 'sound', rather than exist as sound. I stress this aural dimension because it is the popular way into his verse, and quite properly so.

All poets write to purge something in themselves, to find out what lives in their own minds. But professional poets (and good ones), in wrestling with their own turbulence, smooth the path for their public. Out of many grim preoccupations Dannie Abse finds a reasoned and haunting poetry, and I don't believe that he is able to do so just because of high idealism or intellect—rather it seems that the need for memorable and musical poetry has pushed him into the endless fight with words. In this way, the clever devices of 'Letter to *The Times*,' which I probably failed to find sufficiently jocular on early acquaintance, bemused by what seemed their daring strategy, have been naturalised for me by my knowing and hearing the rest of Abse's poetry, by a sort of baptism through sound, a loving extension of the pleasure principle to human edginess.

The poetry thus existed in my consciousness before the man, but I do remember the first time the man himself impinged on me, because we met in uncharacteristic circumstances—at least they were less characteristic of Dannie than of me. Sometime in 1961 I had been recording a poem with George MacBeth at Broadcasting House, and we went afterwards to the BBC's nearest pub, The George in Mortimer Street. Dannie was at the bar, and was not sober. I think it is the only time I have seen him the worse for drink. My first book of poems had just appeared—*Once Bitten, Twice Bitten*—and I had concurred with the publisher's request for a biographical note by providing a facetious piece I now regret, which described me as 'an unhelpful supporter of the Labour Party' (true still), and added that 'my ambition was to be a playwright.' All I remember of our conversation when I was introduced to Dannie Abse was his stern rebuke to me for wanting to be a playwright when I had already been called to the noblest profession of all, that of poet. There was something prophetic in this and also something ironic. Abse has never swerved from his conviction that the poet, this seemingly uninfluential bender of words, so small a figure beside the celebrated captains of business, science and the academy, has the most important job of all, whether one calls it 'purifying the language of the tribe' or 'providing early warning systems for the psyche of the race.' But it is Abse and not I who has gone on to be the playwright. I can just about compose words for music, for cantatas and operas, but when I try to write for the theatre my characters become obsessional monologuists and the only action is melodrama in the last few minutes.

Dannie Abse's sense of theatre can be perceived in his poetry. He shows great cunning in the manner of his composition of dramatic lyrics. All too many poets today, attracted by the perennial charms of the monologue of character, follow Browning's encylopaedic inclusiveness without enjoying Browning's natural forcefulness and sense of onward movement. Abse never falls into this trap, he never clutters his poems with accruing detail; nor does he take famous figures as his speakers, persons the reader or hearer is bound to know a lot about already and to be interested in from history or anecdote. Consequently, his *Collected Poems* has none of those pieces which were summed-up by Max Beerbohm: 'enter Leonardo da Vinci, Michelangelo, Lorenzo the Magnificent etc, all saying things highly characteristic of themselves.'

Abse's comic creations, his Aunt Alice, his Uncle Isidore, Rabbi Schatz, display the economy and telling humanity of his impersonations at their most succinct, but the justice of his dramatic method is most sharply seen and most extensively portrayed in his sequence 'Funland.' This kind of gallimaufry of psychological horrors and comic-strip archetypes, taking Eliot's 'The whole world is our hospital/Endowed by the ruined millionaire' as its keynote, can all too easily turn into slickness. That it doesn't testifies to Abse's paring-down of case-history, and his dramatic selection of occasions. For so Monty-Python-like a creation, 'Funland' is surprisingly laconic. 'Anybody here seen any Thracians' is a chilling presentation of the sodality of madness. It is easy, reading this second section, to understand how our everyday paranoid tics can flower into group delusion. Abse, here, picks up the idea of exclusion, of the need for enemies and gives it an original gloss:

> *He wanted to found*
> *a Society not a Religion*
> *and a Society he says*
> *washing his hands with moonlight*

> *in a silver bowl*
> *has to be exclusive.*
> *Therefore someone must be banned.*
> *Who? Who? Tell us Pythagoras.*
> *The Thracians yes the Thracians.*

Abse's language is very spare and slender and accommodates the glancing of lyricism without letting it interrupt the poem's progress. The Thracians, of course, will never be tracked-down, since they 'have blue hair and red eyes.' So the totalitarian future is under no threat ´ ·m the rational:

> *Now all day we loiter near the gates*
> *hoping to encounter someone of this description*
> *so that what is now a Religion*
> *can triumphantly become a society.*

This is an apt comment on the secularising of modern life, where even those closest to magic, the mad, lust after the social and mechanical. In all Abse's poetry, the lineaments of society are stressed: he is a poet of townscape, of work, professions, restaurants, holidays, families, voices in gardens, the way we live now. In his verse, the green giant, Nature, edges into the suburbs of North London, but is out-stared. Abse encounters an emblematic questioner at a poetry reading, who asks about English wild flowers, but he can never satisfy her proper concern:

> *But no! Done for in the ignorant suburb,*
> *I'll drink Scotch, neurotically stare through glass*
> *at the rainy lawn, at green stuff, nameless birds,*
> *and let my daughter, madam, go to nature class.*

Much that he deliberates on is seen through suburban windows. The poet looks out at Nature and Society, or looks in through other people's windows at lives which never can be wholly known. He appreciates—and this occurs in poem after poem—that love is real and gentle, but is subject to an endless range of separations, some of them historic and tragic, some social and comic. In Golders Green 'If a light should fly on in an upstairs room / odds on two someones are going to sleep,' while in Soho, 'If a light should fly on in an upstairs

70

room / odds on two someones are going to bed.' In these categories of oddness, the poet is the oddest one of all. He is always noticing, thinking and comparing, aware that his art distances him from the full humanity of his subjects but he is happy to share with them the dilemma of being alive in a palpable world. Abse's sense of this palpableness informs everything he writes.

I have been with Dannie Abse in many different places, and talked with him under several sorts of dispensation, but I always associate him with social happiness, with the conversation of equals in places not yet robbed of their Arcadian spirit. When we were together in Israel, he was perhaps more sombre, as befits a Jew of the Diaspora, but I think he saw more humanity there than we wide-eyed Gentiles did. I was surprised how much of what I took to be biblical in the Sunday School sense lives on in Israel, especially in Samaria. Christianity is a dark legacy for me, and I was seldom undisturbed during our two week stay. It was Dannie who lightened one occasion. We had gone for a swim in the Sea of Galilee (Lake Tiberias in Israeli nomenclature); it was February and the water was cold. Dennis Enright and Ted Hughes were wise enough to stay warm on the bank. As we emerged shivering, Dannie said: 'Now I understand why Christ preferred to walk on the top.' What could never be blasphemy for him had a liberating effect for me. My parents were atheists, albeit Presbyterian and Baptist atheists, but I still manage to find the Church a dark place and Christ a very ambiguous Redeemer. New Testament darkness seemed everywhere in Israel. Dannie was able to see the idealism of the Jewish state: most of what I saw was Western European technology. But while his recent poetry has included many witty and wise embroideries on traditional rabbinical stories (themselves like more humane versions of Zen absurdity), Dannie Abse's work is more English in tone than Jewish. He strikes me as a quintessentially English writer, and I mean English and not Welsh. Hearing him read his popular poem, 'Not Adlestrop,' in his resonant voice, the detail, the tone and the quietness of feeling amount to a conjuration of heartland England. The doctor turned poet (or I think I should write the poet who trained as a doctor) is another strengthening of his English connection. His pastoral duties have taken him into many insalubrious places and shown him despair in many lives. I think they have reinforced that humanity which critics have always recognized as his hallmark. The doctor, priest and presider over life and death, is the central observer in a number of his poems. One which arises directly from medical practice and gives him an excellent metaphor is 'The Stethoscope.' After celebrating the instrument as sounding chamber of birth (on a pregnant woman's abdomen) and death (inside the chest of a corpse), Abse ends his poem with a paean of secular praise, his alternative to the litany of priest or rabbi.

> *I should*
> *by doing so celebrate my own ears,*
> *by praising them praise speech at midnight*
> *when men become philosophers;*
> *laughter of the sane and insane;*
>
> *night cries*
> *of injured creatures, wide-eyed or blind;*
> *moonlight sonatas on a needle;*
> *lovers with doves in their throats; the wind*
> *travelling from where it began.*

Doctors are proverbially well placed to practice humanism, but they have to find strictness in order to avoid mere empathy. Abse, as poet, belongs to the end of the medical spectrum which is grouped round Chekhov: he is an artist, not an anecdotist like Maugham and Cronin. He quotes at the start of his *Collected Poems* that (to my taste) over-used credo of W. C. Williams, 'No ideas but in things,' and he certainly enjoys Williams's ability to notice and select salient physical details in his verse. But Abse is in the English and not the American vein. Thomas Hardy was a great noticer of things, but also a great moulder of ideas and notions. Abse's poetry, like Hardy's, seems to me to be full of 'ideas,' and I like it the better for that. Paradoxically, American poetry is chilled by its 'thinginess'; it becomes inhuman in its drive for classicism. English poetry, ready to indulge impurity in art by thinking aloud, is warmer and more human. It is perhaps time for a return to sententiousness. With Dannie Abse, the sententious wears its humanity lightly.

I mentioned earlier Abse's unrivalled use of the refrain in poetry. But musicality is stitched into his verse in ways more subtle than obvious recurrence. His repetitions often occur in the middle of stanzas or irregularly at points where they startle. In this he advances beyond Louis MacNeice, another master of refrain-writing.

In the comic poem, 'Miss Book World,' the line 'not that we are, but they imagine us so,' moves, enlarging its irony, through the following two stanzas, with only the relevant change of pronoun. But the effect on the poem is to turn a fairly ordinary, lightly satirical piece into something haunting, a touch liturgical. The child-like snatches of phrase which we carry with us from nursery rhymes are made use of in Abse's poetry, since he recognizes that language is ritual and mystery as well as communication and analysis. 'Hunt the Thimble,' one of my favourites of his work, is packed with old instances and adages, the children's party game becoming a not-too-heavily-underlined metaphor for menace, the true end of everything. 'You cannot describe it' he writes. 'You are cold, altogether too cold.' Even in the shared warmth of a poetry reading, the secondary meaning of this sentence is frightening. Perhaps if we were not so cold, in the deepest sense, we might find the thimble. If so, alas, it would be on the finger of Atropos, as she cuts the thread.

From Funland to Funland! An ellipse

GIGLIOLÁ SACERDOTI MARIANI

The study of a poet's work normally begins with early work but I wish to start and end with 'Funland.' Firstly, because I believe 'Funland' to be Abse's masterpiece where his art appears at its most daring and assured; secondly, because a number of Abse's earlier and later themes, symbols and allegories—from those in *Tenants of the House* (1957) to his most recent collection of poems, *Way Out in the Centre* (1981)—are resumed or prefigured in this long poem; thirdly, because, through it, one can hint at the fundamental unity of Abse's works (poetry, theatre, prose)—at his unified sensibility.

His experience as writer and doctor finds in 'Funland' a richer expression than hitherto. Effectively exploiting the potentialities of the common use language, the colloquial syntax, the common rhythm of the phrases, he employs—through a more complex imagery—the homely and the esoteric in close, intense, witty juxtaposition. Although 'Funland' is, on an intellectual level, hard to comprehend, there is a massive emotional directness in it that one comes across. If we agree with T. S. Eliot's 'genuine poetry can communicate before it is understood' we may add that 'Funland' communicates something it has in common with dreams. For dreams also, as Freud puts it, 'think in images.'

Abse has said of 'Funland' that 'it is *The Waste Land* gone mad': it is a desolate land, a civilization more savage, more psychotic than that described by T. S. Eliot; and in the introduction to his play, *Pythagoras*—which derives directly from 'Funland'—Abse recalls that Freud once remarked to Wilhelm Reich, 'the whole of humanity is my patient.' He recalls also a conversation he had with Elias Canetti who said to him, 'The man suffering from paranoia is correct. Someone *is* standing behind that door pumping invisible gas through the keyhole. For we are dying, right now, a little every minute.' Abse in that introduction adds little else. To explain or comment on 'Funland,' he believes, would be to rationalize it *post hoc*, or to develop a kind of personal mythology out of it. Abse believes the poem must explain itself and that, besides, in every genuine literary creation each line means more than its author knows. 'Every poem of mine which I think works'—he told me recently—'contains much more than I thought I had put in it. Indeed you have sensed, perceived, *something* in the lines which I had not realized was there and that now I discover with you.'

Behind the euphemistic title of 'Funland'—which because of its intricate symbolic-cultural structure may be considered the most cryptic and esoteric creation in Abse's *Collected Poems*—we find the surrealistic description of a mental hospital, in microcosm the society in which we live: wild atmosphere, absurd relationships, mazes of passions, voices from other worlds, fragments of life. An enunciating 'I' introduces, in the first three movements of the poem, all the essential *dramatis personae* that inhabit Funland: the Superintendent; a patient 'whom the Superintendent has nicknamed Pythagoras'; and then further patients, Blondie, Marian, and an 'atheist uncle.' All these creatures find themselves part of a natural disorder along with 'black-garbed priests' and 'scientists in long white coats.'

The enunciating 'I', though psychically torn or dissociated like the others, is the fulcrum of every action. He is the unitary element of 'Funland.' He seems to guide the itinerary of a collective madness. This reaches, in the second movement, its climax in a kind of hallucinatory, ambiguous initiation where Dionysiac and Pythagorean rites mix with primitive taboos and false modern ones through an ironical anachronistic syncretism: 'Members promise to abstain / from swallowing beans. They promise / not to pick up what has fallen / never to stir a fire with an iron / never to eat the heart of animals / never to walk on motorways / never to look in a mirror / that hangs beside a light.' (*CP*, 165) Vivid visual passages are summoned up in the third movement by a return to mythological expressions and by images—immediate, pervasive and haunting—which while suggesting an eerie menace, are also humorous:

> *At once the scientists take off*
> *the priests hurry up*
> *into the sky. They zoom.*
> *They free-wheel high over roof tops*
> *playing guitars;*
> *they perform exquisite*
> *figures of 8*
> *but the old mediocre reprobate*
> *merely shrinks them*
> *then returns to his smelly coffin.*
> *Slowly winking he pulls down the lid*
> *slowly the coffin sinks into the ground.*
> *(Bye brighteyes! Arrivederci brighteyes!)*
>
> (CP, 168)

The return to the mythological and those images of indefinite sensation, strikingly phantasmagorical, introduce the fourth movement where the effect is not visual but aural: 'Coughing and echo of echoes. / A lofty resonant public place. / It is the assembly hall. / Wooden chairs on wooden planks.' (CP, 169) Verbal communication is fictitious. All the 'inhabitants' of Funland are incapable of communicating—including a poet who reads, or tries to read, his own poetry devoid of content: 'He is an underground vatic poet. / His purple plastic coat is enchanting. / Indeed he is chanting / 'Fu-er-uck Fu-er-uck'. / with spiritual concentration.' (CP, 169).

All the 'patients' mime plausible identities to escape from their own 'diversity'; they offer simulacra of themselves to exorcise the mutilations of their bodies, the loss of their own identities (body and mind are all one thing wrapped up by a hostile world): 'Fat Blondie stands inconsolable / in the middle of the goldfish pool. / She will not budge. / The musky waters have amputated her feet.' (CP, 176) They draw near to the verge of the total nihil, but, owing to a kind of subtle self-deceit, they see only the contours of evil, protected as they are by 'black glasses': 'As a result my atheist uncle / has fitted black lenses / into his spectacles. They are so opaque / he cannot see through them. / . . . There are rumours that next week / all of us will be issued with black specs.' (CP, 172, 173) All human beings experience self-deceit and irrationality. The tension between blindness and vision, between light and dark, reaches its climax in the lines 'a blind poet / reading Homer' (*CP*, 172). The oxymoron (the sight-giving semantic component is subordinate to the sight-denying one) underlines the incapacity to see both physically and intellectually, since lack of sight combines with lack of reason.

The realistic elements, sensual and sexual, interplay with surrealist suggestions that break any trace of logical connection between thoughts; the fight between Eros and Thanatos develops and spreads out in a turgid metaphoric vortex. The 'atheist uncle' 'retires' to the silent geometry of the pillar box while Marian and Blondie display their repressed sexuality: 'Marian eyeing the bard / maintains he is a real / sexual messiah / that his poem was not an expletive / but an incitement. / Fat Blondie cannot cease from crying. / She thinks his poem so nostalgic.' (*CP*, 170) Moreover we perceive that death instinct is evoked in every downward movement and libido in every upward-going element: 'Look how spitting on his hands first / he climbs the flagpole. / Wild at the very top he shouts / I AM IMMORTAL.' (*CP*, 177) Indeed, moral problems and conflicts take on a scenic dimension without any special or temporal connection—the monologue becomes a dialogue or perhaps an eternal delirium, because the others are only the proliferating shadows of the enunciating 'I'. Empiric time and space are replaced by inner time and space.

Initially even the landscape is a maze of objects, of refuse that becomes threatening:

> *A harp with the nerves missing*
> *the somewhat rusty*
> *sheet iron wings of an angel*
> *a small bent tubular hoop*
> *still flickering flickering*
> *like fluorescent lighting*
> *when first switched on*
> *that old tin lizzie banger*
> *Elijah's burnt-out chariot*
> *various other religious hardware*
> *and to cap it all*
> *you may not believe this*
> *a red Edwardian pillar box.*

(*CP*, 163)

In that overstuffed disorder bewilderment is ontological and deontological. One needs certainties: thus the moment of discrimination (where a group of people who are different—with 'blue hair and red eyes'—are threatened with future persecution and diaspora) becomes, paradoxically, the emblematic moment of certainty and cohesion of this society.

The style is intentionally fragmentary—irregular, purposely inconsistent: the rhythm now diffuse, diluted, now dense and concentrated; the stanzas of different lengths split up the images, as in some of Picasso's paintings, to show us how ephemeral are the boundaries between oneiric and real space, between myth and science, between rational and irrational, between sane and unsound minds. The particular graphic solutions—the careful use of capitals and of visual rhythmic pauses; the scanty punctuation marks; the ellipses, logical and grammatical; the assonances; the onomatopoeic words; the alliterations;—all combine to dilate the verbal delirium of a diasporic odyssey: 'Suddenly above us / frightful insane / the full moon breaks free from a cloud / stares both ways / and the stars in their stalls tremble.' (CP, 181)

Simultaneous and multiple echoes, such as Reich's orgonic energy (as opposed to nuclear energy) and Pythagorean harmony (the unity of the manifold, the concordance of discordance) link up with further magical and mythological suggestions of literary allusions to accumulate and interplay and grow into a complex that is rich with intellectual and emotional associations. Through Shakespeare's line, ('we are but shrubs not tall cedars') or the echo of the insane Ophelia's farewell ('Goodbye Blondie, goodbye uncle, goodbye') to precise biblical references to Passover and Elijah ('What about Elijah I asked / . . . Why else each springtime / with the opening of a door / no-one's there?') Abse would lead us to the most frightful lunacy of our century, the Nazi fury: 'smashed smashed years ago like the rest of them / gone with the ravens gone with the lightning.' (CP, 181)

In Funland life is, therefore, characterized by precariousness and opaqueness, it is degraded to absurd nonsense. It is an existence distorted by cold human relationships, cultural consumerism: 'His purple plastic coat is enchanting'; undisputed acquiescence and forced conformism: 'Most of us laugh / because the others are laughing / most of us clap / because the others are clapping.' (CP, 169) Moreover it is an existence warped by the terror of a coercive authority and by the threat of nuclear energy. The only comfort lies in the sweetness of a dream, the only catharsis in fancy, the only redemption in the loving gesture of a hand. The only sanity lies in the conjugation of the verb *to love*, in the first elementary love-words so difficult to express but so capable of reconciling any antinomy: ' "Love read this though it has little meaning / for by reading this you give me meaning" / I wrote or think I wrote or meant to write / and receiving no reply I heard / the silence. . . .' (*CP*, 172)

> *Oh love I write*
> *surely love was no less*
> *because less uttered or more accepted?*
>
> (*CP*, 179)

Then one may stop and say 'Sometimes Funland can be beautiful,' (*CP*, 182), may feel in this statement an affirmative note, a message of reassuring wisdom, and take courage again.

According to some recent theories the 'demons' in ourselves are precious to us. They are part of human existence: if we learn to live with them they may allow us to find a psychic balance that may be called 'eudemonistic morals'. Abse seems to possess this patrimony—'eudemonistic morals'—which enables him to take a balanced view of the positive and negative aspects of life. Before a deceiving world he is watchful observer, anxious and sensitive, one now painfully wise, one now deeply bewildered by and concerned about common reality: 'I start with the visible / and am startled by the visible.' (*CP*, 128) The poet affords the joy of a passionate openness before experience; the doctor is aware of the limits of science, of the inevitable merciful lies of doctors ('Miracles', *CP*, 159; 'A winter visit' and 'The doctor,' *WOC*, 18, 19) and is vulnerable like everyone else ('because when sick I'm still a doctor', *WOC*, 22). He voices the eternal wonder before the miracle of creation at the moment of the scientific and emotional auscultation of the rhythms of life—from the resonant 'The smile was' (*CP*, 121) to the more controlled and calmer mood of 'The stethoscope' (*CP*, 204). He celebrates the events of everyday life, his sufferings and his affections, his being a son and a father. (*CP*, 136; *WOC*, 53)

Some of Abse's poems have an almost visible brilliance; they involve the senses and the feelings equally and strongly. Through the powerful impact of his tropes Abse makes us see pogroms and concentration camps, taste the bitter irony of Yiddish tales, hear the sad music of the *shtetl* life and the aphorisms of apocryphal rabbis. (*CP*, 194, 195; *WOC*, 26, 28) His metaphors are quite daring: they throw two particles of the world so surprisingly and accurately upon each other that, for the reader's imagination, they become one; as in the second part of 'Ghosts, Angels, Unicorns,' that is dedicated to the angelical species: Most are innocent, shy, will not undress. / They own neither genitals nor pubic hair. / Only the fallen of the hierarchy / make an appearance these secular days. // No longer useful as artists' models, / dismissed by theologians, morale tends / to be low—even high-class angels grumble / as they loiter in our empty churches. (*CP*, 184) Almost completely without a surprising use of words, the two images—the one sensual, the other spiritual—convey the idea of the endless ambiguity of existence, allude to the transitoriness of things, displaying ironic humour, and are also balanced in what Arnold called poetry's two 'interpretations'—natural magic and moral profundity.

Indeed, in most of his poems, Abse links tale to confession, gnomic statement to uninhibited expression; he finds the exact, humorous, colloquial accent to be joined to his esoteric language.

In some of his earlier poems—'The trial' (*CP*, 17), 'The ballad of Oedipus Sex' (*CP*, 100)—polyphonic stanzas and throbbing rhythms counterpoint dramatic images, while reiterations or refrains, indicate and determine a development of themes to give the poet the certainty of a formal discipline. In his most recent compositions, too, the duality of tone, or rather the dichotomy between form and content, may be emblematic not only of a deep personal conflict, but also of emotional involvement and empathy. 'Cousin Sidney' is one such poem. Here Abse constructs a series of stanzas mainly in monosyllables—which provide the necessary control to the shifting emotion—without giving an effect of monotony; besides, the verbid 'unswinging' (one of the two words in the whole poem that are more than a disyllable) which conveys the idea of stillness, states as it were, the theme itself of the poem—death.

Actually, the variety of the diction, the union of the common word and the more formal one ('Through it / over young women's abdomens tense, / I have heard the sound of creation / and in a dead man's chest, the silence / before creation began.'), the conver-

sational and the remote ('Should I / kneel before it, chant an apoph-
thegm / from a small text? Mimic priest or rabbi, / the swaying
noises of religious men? / Never! Yet I could praise it.'), the precise
and the suggestive ('night cries / of injured creatures, wide-eyed or
blind; / moonlight sonatas on a needle; / lovers with doves in their
throats; the wind / travelling from where it began.') is made possible by the flexibility of the metres that Abse uses. Besides, all the
above quoted lines—from 'The stethoscope' (*CP*, 204)—show us
that Abse's poetry is made of men, not of things or fetishes. 'Creative attention'—as Simone Weil wrote—'means really giving our
attention to what does not exist. Humanity does not exist in the
anonymous flesh lying inert by the roadside.' Such is the quality of
Abse's concern; he makes himself and his readers human in that
sense by his creative attention. 'Writing poetry is an immersion into
common reality not an escape from it,' (*PIF*, 198) he observes; and
he portrays life in its transparent gestures and simple details never
trying to escape the obduracy of people, things and situations, but
with an intellectual tautness often associated with a quiet irony,
expressing instead the complexity of human contradictions—in
poetry, prose and theatre, from *Ash on a Young Man's Sleeve* and
Poems, Golders Green to *Dogs of Pavlov* and from 'Funland' to
Pythagoras.

The episodes which in his prose works provide material for comedy are deeply explored in the poems and bring forth a transformation of memory into vision. Indeed the single poems become more
intelligible in the light of the compositions belonging to the same
collection and each collection opens up to new possible interpretations when examined in the entire context of the Absean production—which is an organically interrelated whole. Moreover, if, on
one hand, the familiarity with the stage helps Abse, in his poetry, to
shape a scene, to sketch characters and present dialogue, on the
other hand, in his plays, he manages to combine his prose gift for
humorous fantasy based on realistic observation with his poetic gift
of evocative language.

The Dogs of Pavlov is one such play. It is based upon the well-
known psychological experiment carried out during the 1960s by
Professor Stanley Milgram at Yale University and exhibits once
more the close connection existing for Abse between his medical
professional concern and his literary works. Abse uses the experiment—which was devised to show how far people would go in

obeying evil commands—as a point of departure: he questions human guinea-pig experiments, denounces manipulation of power and racial prejudice while pointing out the dangers of conforming—political and / or cultural—submission.

The play itself, dense, absorbing, engaging, both for the performer and for the audience is, in the ordinary sense, dramatic: the characters are confronted with moral choices. So is the audience. At one point the enfolding drama mounts to a great poetic climax—in a dream scene where the characters become caricatures of themselves and where literary allusions and references (to *Macbeth*, *Sweeney Agonistes*, *The Waste Land* and to Martin Luther King's speech 'I have a dream,') together with key-words reiterated, suggest ominous signs of an oncoming violence and death—despite a comical and satirical surface. A primitive religious rite is suggested, the rite of obedience: 'Trust me. Pull the black lever. Pull the black lever. Pull the black lever. Trust me. Kill the nigger lover. Kill the nigger lover. Trust us. Kill the nigger lover.' (*DOP*, 99)

One feels the sincerity of Abse's deontological concerns and appreciates his language that keeps the flavour and the dimension of everyday life, even when he blends medical terms and poetical tropes in the realistic dialogue of his characters.

But the close relationship between his gifts for poetry and theatre, his unified sensibility—as I defined it at the beginning of this essay—is most obviously illustrated in the connection between 'Funland' and his play *Pythagoras*. The images and symbols of 'Funland' recur here, their meaning deepened or expanded by new associations, by their new treatment on the stage. Most of the characters too are the same. They inhabit a mental home; they have gone through the torment of unaccepted or unreciprocated love, and the isolation that ensues; they have gone through the horror of life stripped of all illusion. There is one Tony Smith—a former stage magician—who believes himself to be Pythagoras reincarnated. He thinks he has supernatural powers. He can make telephones ring from a distance with a simple motion of his hand; summon up thunder and lightning by uttering puzzling Greek sentences and order even the celestial spheres to play magic harmonies with the help of a wand.

Facts are reduced to the least, to the advantage of an emotional and evocative concentration. A series of ludicrous misunderstandings and witty remarks—that contribute to the loosening of ten-

sion—edge the play towards its climax, towards the demonstra-
tion-show that the patients are forced to perform in front of medical students. If, in that scene—and in the whole play—doctors try
to reduce every individual to a stereotyped homogeneity, Tony
Smith, in believing himself Pythagoras may be trying to express his
own frustrated intellectual ambitions or the fascination that mystical
experience arouses in him. He tries to define what is perhaps a
universal predicament: 'human kind cannot bear very much reality.'
Also, that human kind should rediscover, re-establish an association
of the Pythagorean kind, where religious ethics and science together
might lead to a moral reform of society.

The subject may seem distressing, but there are moments of
subtle humour, to prove that 'the insane startle us with their searing
truths' (PY, II), to point out how schizophrenia and paranoia may
affect the so-called sane people, and how the genial lucid madness of
Pythagoras is preferable to the hyper-rationalism in which scientists
get lost as in the following dialogue: 'SUPERINTENDENT—You
don't think that, because of your . . . breakdown . . . you imagine
that you are Pythagoras? PYTHAGORAS—No, it is because I'm
Pythagoras restored to this discordant century that I've had a breakdown.' (PY, 31)

The songs of a patient, Arthur, the poetic compositions and the
curious formulae of Pythagoras scan the rhythm of the momentous
scenes and extend the narrative time of the play. Pythagoras, with
his mood and manner—mystical, magic and metaphysical—with
his alchemies and philosophical intuitions is the magician of the
play and, in one sense, its producer.

'Don't call him Pythagoras. His name is Tony Smith' (PY, 80)
may be considered the concluding line of Pythagoras and 'Do not
wake us. We may die' (CP, 183) is the last line of 'Funland.' The two
lines, in spite of their apparent discrepancy, are coterminous. In
fact, where does the imagination of reality end and where does the
reality of imagination begin? We cannot answer. We should rather
quote what Dylan Thomas wrote in a letter dated 1938: 'The poem
is, as all poems are, its own question and answer, its own contradiction, its own agreement. . . The aim of a poem is the mark that the
poem itself makes: it's the bullet and the bull's eye; the knife, the
growth and the patient. A poem moves only towards it own end,
which is the last line.' And the last line of 'Funland' may seem a
contradiction, but it is also an agreement. It is the final chorus, to

83

which the resonance of the line 'Till human voices wake us and we drown' from 'The Love Song of J. Alfred Prufrock' may provide contrast and counterpoint.

The inhabitants of Funland do not want to leave their reverie, because with their vision, fancy, dream, they can build a new dimension of life, devise an *ubi consistam*, a human immortality.

The Plays of Dannie Abse: Responsibilities

JOHN CASSIDY

'In dreams begins responsibility,' used by Yeats as the epigraph to his 1914 volume, could stand also at the head of all Dannie Abse's published plays. From the first performance of *House of Cowards* in 1960 to that of *Gone in January* in 1977, their dramatic images have been concerned with the making of choices and with the recognition of moral imperatives. Though differing considerably in setting, technique and achievement, the plays are obviously linked, obviously the products of the same imagination.

These plays are aloof from the main currents moving through English theatre in the sixties and seventies, which in itself awakens sympathetic curiosity. If they have an affinity to anything outside themselves it is perhaps to the radio play, that underestimated form in which reliance upon language is often virtually complete. That is not to say that Abse's plays lack theatricality, as we shall see, but it is an indication of how much his language achieves in this context. A reader of his poetry will know that Dannie Abse has an ear for the rhythms of the speaking voice, and this link between his poetry and his plays is at once evident. The people who inhabit these dramas, whatever their status as characters, whatever the nature of their interests, are people whose lines are eminently speakable. They are, to that extent, convincing.

The Questors Theatre of Ealing, through its annual Festival of New Plays, was responsible for the commissioning and presentation of the early plays later collected and published by Scorpion Press as *Three Questor Plays*. The first of these, *House of Cowards* (1960), is of a kind which frequently occurs in the radio schedules, centring upon a family living in a modest corner house in an anonymous town. The family has its crotchety father, long-suffering mother and mildly rebellious son; alongside them are two eccentric lodgers and the son's rather ordinary fiancée. It seems like the world of the everyday radio play, with quirky characters and lively back-chat, well-written and well-designed. The familiarity reassures, perhaps intentionally mis-leads, the audience, especially as it is never completely dissipated but continues as an element in the play till the end.

The anonymity is conventional, too, and extends to the central mystery, the identity of the strange Speaker who is to visit the town. He is hailed by some as an evangelist, by others as a politician, according to their own proclivities. It is necessary to the play that he remains unidentifiable, so that he can act as a projection of the personality of each of those expecting him, and even the journalist who is assigned to be his forerunner is far from precise about him. The danger is that this uncertainty could be overdone, that this kind of anonymity could become in itself too obvious and pervasive, leading to a loss of energy. Abse avoids this by concentrating on the concreteness of certain details, both in the set which is carefully described in the stage directions, and in the dialogue. Hicks, the father, remembers a litany of pre-war makes of bicycle, the journal-ist recalls well-known press stories of the fifties, and Mrs Hicks lists the names of the Hollywood stars of her youth. They live in a recognisably real world, and the disturbing unknown is thereby isolated, emphasised and located in the figure of The Speaker.

The build-up to The Speaker's arrival is carefully managed, so that at the same time we have an unfolding of the characters involved, establishing them as unsettled and dissatisfied, lives ready for a transforming revelation, or at least waiting for something to happen. They are ordinary yet extraordinary, like most people, each with a distinct identity and ambition, even if the ambition is only to be left alone. They seem at first the sort of people we have met before in plays, the married couple living in tolerant animosity, the male lodger with his sexual boasting, the old maid whose fiancé was tragically killed years previously, the moderately ambitious son. These identities are fixed quickly, in an economic and workmanlike way. When it seems as if The Speaker's arrival is imminent, indeed that he has chosen this house as his lodging, they approach the possibility in sharply individual ways. Hicks is at first sceptical, even hostile, but is won over by the bait of a thousand pounds. His wife is flattered and flustered. Miss Avery, the spinster, is overcome by religious exhilaration. The son George is drawn by the atmosphere of excited enthusiasm onto the streets, and Alf the lodger is fired by a naive hope for political change.

Once we accept the unlikely circumstance that, for all the prepublicity and the razzmatazz, no one is sure what The Speaker is or what he looks like, we know that in the world of this play nothing is quite what it seems. Any precedent for this kind of visit to a fifties town, from a current Eastern guru or a charismatic politician, cannot be a very relevant precedent; so that when George and his fiancée meet a stranger apparently about to throw himself off a bridge, the identity of the stranger is at once suspect. Is he what his circumstances and his conversation suggest, a recently discharged mental patient, or is he going to reveal himself as The Speaker? The ambiguity of the scene is nicely judged, and its dramatic effect considerable when the stranger poises himself on the parapet as the train screams past below—but does not jump. A failed suicide, wanting courage, a polite, humble man, this Mr Nott can also speak about challenges, decisions and self-deception; his language is in a different register from that of the others; he is mysterious. George is echoing the audience's reaction when he half suggests to him that he is The Speaker.

The ambiguity is never fully resolved. In a powerful scene in the house Mr Nott is revealed as the convalescent he claims to be, instead of the visitant who will change the lives of all he meets. He is not The Speaker. And yet in a way, of course, he is. In the terms of the story he is simply the well-named Mr Nott, but in the cataclysmic effect of his visit he is something else. Referring to his own humble identity he asks the others to face the truth, and amid the extreme tensions generated this is what they do. They suddenly face the truth about themselves and one another. The spinster's fiancé, so far from having died heroically, had been an unsatisfactory lover for a brief time in her past, a married man with four children who had slunk out of her life. Alf the Don Juan has eyes only for boy scouts. Hicks the invalid is a lead-swinger and a petty thief. But it does not last. The wounds close, the defences are rebuilt, and their lives begin again as if there had been nothing, no moment of revelation. It is an honest and sobering conclusion.

Yet the effect of the play is not dispiriting. What lingers is what has made the most dramatic impact, the words of Mr Nott. He preaches—that must be the word—acceptance, realism and a trust in the future. He is the optimist in a hostile world. He asks for courage, for if his listeners had it they 'wouldn't have to search for any public orthodoxy, or build a cocoon of dreams, or any false structure to feel safe in . . . there'd be just the green, cruel ordinary world that indisputably is, and you'd praise that difficult simplicity.' He is distinguished and isolated by his different language as well as by his propositions and his earnestness. As one of the triumvirate of lunatic, lover and poet he has, privileged by literary tradition, access to special insights. He is more than Mr Nott, and the drama lies in the collision between him and the shabby pretences of everyone else. What he wants them to accept is not things as they are, but responsibility.

This early play repays investigation because it contains so much of what the later work develops. We find a central ambiguity, something of a mystery, the deliberate use of linguistic variety, a delight in strong theatrical effects, and the maintenance of some of the norms of conventional plays as a kind of telling irony, all of which become familiar later on. A Mr Nott figure, too, reappears, notably in *Pythagoras*. Most clearly of all we have the forcing, out of apparently unlikely material, of attention to ways of living lives.

The second Questor play is the one-act *Gone* (1962), later extended to three acts and published in *Madog* by the Polytechnic of Wales. In this form it was given an extended run at the Young Vic in 1978, after appearing the year before at the Edinburgh Festival, with the title *Gone in January*. At one-act length it is so resonant and complete that the extension courts disappointment, but the additional acts are a genuine development and *Gone in January* is a very interesting play indeed. The quadrangular affair, among a weak husband, his wife and two weak other men, unfolds not so much as a plot as a series of bizarre episodes. Act 1 is a two-hander, beginning promisingly with an apparent preparation for suicide and an immediate intruder through the window. The conversation which forms the act, strange, sad and comical at once, maintains an admirable tautness and presents very fully a complexity involving the husband Peter, Aubrey the intrudent (who is present), Connie the wife and Tony Pickerall, evidently the latest lover, (who are only mentioned). It ends with Peter's head in the noose once more, either in despairing suicide or another self-deceiving gesture.

In the extended version, Connie and Tony both appear, and there is a new element arising from Peter's African masks and his interest in magic. The mystery and ambiguity hover all the time—Peter's magic is explicable as that of a leg-pulling ventriloquist, yet there seem to be other possibilities. The incantations work, and their power is dismissed only with a certain unease. This play is full of oddities, of speech, behaviour and situation, so that the entertainment never flags. It is comedy of the bizarre rather than the Absurd, without existentialist *angst* or any feeling of willed pointlessness. The dialogue is too witty for that, and the comedy too humane. The characters blunder against one another's lives in a bemused way, unwilling to face themselves or accept the full burden of any relationship.

Connie, though she is in the last act only, is in some ways the centre of gravity. She is given several pertinent Rilkean lines, in one case on the nature of possession: 'They say my wife my child my dog and know that all they have called their own, wife, child and dog, remain alien and unknown.' As in the speeches of Mr Nott, the language is alien to the norm of the play, foregrounded by its formality. She speaks too of her longstanding wish for a child: 'I've never told you how often I dream I'm touching the fontanelle of a baby's head. I'm out of touch with something elemental and eternal.' The lines point up the contrast between this imagined fundamental value and the grown-up child she has as a husband, between the genuinely elemental and eternal and Peter's dabblings in dubious magic. Connie is a confused character, but she has a knack of bringing in reminders of other levels of sensibility. Among a number of strange anecdotes which occur in the play, seemingly irrelevant but resonating rather like images in poetry, is an intriguing one from Connie, about

> . . . how some musicians . . . played and a great group moved in dance and in accordance with the beat of the music. Then a deaf man came by who knew nothing of dancing nor of music. So he thought 'How stupid these men are who beat with their fingers on all kinds of implements and those who turn and twist this way and that.'

It is a nice image of incomprehension, of how we are apt to assess the stupidity of others, of how it is possible, like the people in this play, to live on different non-intersecting planes of consciousness. The downbeat ending, when Connie leaves with Tony, and Peter, alone on stage, pops the balloons one by one, is an ending but not a solution. Any solution would have been false, but this last scene has an inevitability which has been worked towards from the beginning.

The four characters in *Gone in January* are not more than sentimentally concerned for one another. *In the Cage* (1964) on the other hand, the third Questor play of nearly fifteen years earlier, is wholly involved with selflessness and interdependence. Prompted by an incident in a Balzac short story, the play is set in an occupied country. We are back with the kind of anonymity found in *A House of Cowards*; the country is unnamed and the time unspecified. The nature of the occupying power is uncertain, as are the politics of the oppressed nationalists. A background like this has so many similarities to past and present situations that the anonymity does not seem specious, nor a get-out which avoids the pressure of historical or political circumstance. It is here a justifiable means of examining human reactions to the exercise of power, wherever found and by whomever controlled. The nature of the international quarrel is not relevant, and what we have presented on stage and investigated is the exercise of power—whether by terrorists who will kill randomly or the authorities who kill selectively and arbitrarily.

The central figures are David the committed activist and the Captain who is the executive agent of oppression. David is responsible for the terrorist killings. Ironically, it is his family which is arbitrarily seized and executed in reparation. His pacifist brother Chris, after various soul-searchings within the family, accepts the responsibility of being himself the executioner—to save other families from the same fate. The Captain, ordered to carry out this extraordinary procedure devised by his General, searches his soul too but eventually acquiesces. There are thus two sets of debates, that within David's family and that between the Captain and the General. The first of these looks back to *Gone*, the second looks forward to *The Dogs of Pavlov*.

The relationships within the victimised family are fairly complex. David and Chris are initially at loggerheads, impatient with each other because possessed of opposing visions. 'I can't be like him,' says David. 'He walks between people gently as if carrying a jug of water full right to the brim.' This is an expressive image of the carefulness—in every sense—of Chris, and also of David's irritation

90

with his brother's inaction. 'Somebody had to do something,' is his rather obvious statement of his own position. Later the tensions force them both into self-questioning, and they worry about guilt and responsibility and the values they live by. Their war-widowed sister Ruth has known love and has an almost mystical attitude towards it, justifying her whole life by reference to that experience. Marcia, attached to both brothers, lives by loyalty to the cause. The father and mother are fatalistic, when not naively hopeful, but quietly defiant and dignified in death.

All of them are compelled by the imminent execution to recognise responsibilities to one another and to other families outside the circle of their own. The final, hideous responsibility—of becoming the executioner—falls by an inexorable dramatic logic to Chris. David's life has been full of violence already, but he will not accept this final act. 'You needed violence, you always have done,' is Chris's accusation, and the pathetic vehemence of David's denial carries his recognition of its truth. Their mother clinches it: 'You must survive this, Chris.' It is a significant line, though the ending of the play belies it.

Chris does survive but, not unexpectedly, in a state of disintegration. The ending is sour. After the terrible sacrifice, those saved by it live on unperturbed. The spectators of the execution attend a dance in the evening, with the soldiers. Tragedy strikes only its direct victims, apparently. As in Auden's 'Musée des Beaux Arts,' those who have seen something amazing have somewhere to get to and sail calmly on. The Captain, mindful of a promotion due, tears up the report on the incident he had intended to forward to the Field Marshal. The final stage direction is chilling: *His face is utterly expressionless*. He too will sail calmly on.

Interdependence, obligation to others, the exercise of humanity, are one aspect of this play. The other concerns the origins of the sense of duty, interpreted as obedience. There is the Captain's appeal to orders, familiar since Nuremberg. He had no choice, he claims; condemning him would be to condemn his superiors, the politicians, the nation. He is merely the agent, and another agent would be found were he to refuse the order. But Chris pushes him beyond this rationalisation. For Chris, the habit of obedience itself, obedience to a father however interpreted, is an ingrained and dehumanising flaw. 'I am saying that we are but children when we obey such commandments, and like children do not feel responsible. I am asking you to feel responsible.' He echoes this later, after the execution, and again stresses the dependence of the child upon the orders of the father: 'You can't expect a child to feel responsible.' Responsibility, then, is maturity, and achieving it is the vital mark of humanity.

The Dogs of Pavlov (1972) pursues this idea relentlessly. Based upon the Yale experiments of Professor Stanley Milgram, the play entered the public arena of controversy surrounding them. Milgram had devised a system whereby volunteers delivered electric shocks to a captive victim (apparently one of themselves but actually a trained actor), in response to arithmetical 'mistakes' on the part of the victim. The experiment was explained as an investigation into the learning process. The switches were dummy switches and the victim's reactions simulated, but this was not known to the volunteers. Milgram's disconcerting discovery was that, whatever the increasing severity of the supposed shocks, and whatever tensions were displayed by the volunteers, none of them refused to continue. To 'help the experiment' they obeyed the orders of the experimenter in charge.

There are profound implications here, which Abse discusses in an essay published with the play, together with Professor Milgram's replies. Important as they are in themselves, particularly concerning the morality of the deception, they do serve to distract attention from what the play itself actually is and how it works. *The Dogs of Pavlov* is, of course, a fictional artifact, not a documentary account nor a tract. As Abse writes, 'I was more interested in how these fictional characters related to each other in human terms rather than in any abstract idea—even if that idea was about the destructive consequences of obedience.'

The play is therefore more complex than the experiment at the centre of it. The people involved are not strangers, to one another or to us. We are made to know them before they begin. Harley-Hoare is the mild, unassuming man who agrees to help because of the extra cash. Sally is the actress hired to represent the victim, a pert, complicated young woman with an off-stage life and a lover, Kurt, half-German, of whom she is not absolutely sure. Not unnaturally, she hates the volunteers, who press the switches thinking she is really in agony. As one of life's victims anyway, she has little trust in her fellow creatures, and hopes only in Kurt.

With hints at the mythical tradition, she sets up a test for Kurt before she will agree to marry him. She inveigles him into becoming a volunteer for the experiment, without revealing her own role in it. Kurt, however, learns of the deception and denounces the whole procedure, attacking both the inhumanity of the experimenters and the deceitfulness of Sally, whom he promptly leaves. She, victim to the end, is left alone on stage, in despair.

The ideological content of the play, if it can be called that, is expressed in this final, climactic scene. Kurt is given powerful denunciatory lines, and his 'Fraud is not research' is forthright and pointed. He accuses the doctors of wanting to luxuriate in their power, 'with the excuse that it's for the fatherland. The fatherland of Science.' The reference is not only to the Nazis but to the habit of filial obedience arraigned in *In the Cage*. The effect is to force attention yet again onto this topic; it is an accusation but not a solution, not a prescription but a plea for awareness of the danger.

Between this play and its predecessors there is a distinct qualitative step. The language has altogether more bounce and colour, and is simply more *convincing*, than anything which has preceded it. With *The Dogs of Pavlov, Pythagoras* and *Gone in January*, Dannie Abse's stage dialogue has attained a different level of vibrancy, without losing any of the colloquial ease of the earlier plays. And with the strength of the dialogue goes a flair for staging which produces at least two events, Sally's dream and the experiment itself, of outstanding theatrical impact. The dream-scene, important thematically, is surreal and ritualistic, isolated in style from the rest of the play. It represents, of course, the inside of Sally's head, and the confusion of insight and triviality, common to dreams, expresses her turmoil in a concretely imagistic way. The mounting of the experiment, with the voltage indicated by coloured lights trained on the victim, punctuated by her pleas and screams, and the crescendo of tension in the operator matched by that in the audience, is extraordinary. There is provision for film interludes, which the author insists should be lyrical to assist in bleeding off tension. The film, of Sally and her previous lover in a London park, would if used throw even further dramatic weight onto the laboratory scene with its flashing lights, shouted orders and cries.

Chary of the prejudice against poets in the theatre, Abse did not reveal at the time that *House of Cowards* had it genesis in a previously published poem, 'The Meeting.' When *Pythagoras* was published in 1979, however, he felt confident enough to include its progenitor, the poem-sequence 'Funland' as an appendix, and a foreword explaining its relationship to the play. It is a close relationship, one of tone, however, rather than of plot. Not the first work to suggest that the world is a madhouse, *Pythagoras* gives us the paradox of the sanity of the insane with a lightness of touch and a poise which guard it from accusations of speciousness. There is an obvious controlling intelligence in command of the play, avoiding any heavy polemicising from a too-simple stance, and fragmenting the humdrum into glittering fragments and surreal episodes. Pythagoras, the central figure, is both patient and healer, both subject and ruler, both mental case and magician. In his person he closes the dichotomies. Compared with others around him he has an enviable wholeness, or at least is aware of and striving for such wholeness. Presenting himself as a reincarnation of the Greek philosopher, he claims a status between mortal and divine. In the reality of the hospital he is a second-rate stage magician with delusions, but this level of reality is continually brought into question. His magic *works*, and though rational explanations are readily available, there is always the possibility, the subtly induced hope, that he really has access to dark and pristine powers.

The dramatic form triumphs here; the audience which lives and must live in scientific reality, aligned with the superintendent, is prevailed upon to want more, to wish to believe in the dimension inhabited by Pythagoras. To court irrationality is dangerous; it is to tread the edge of the abyss. Yet the abyss itself—'we are all dreaming of the abyss'—is made to seem something that must be braved, a necessary reminder of the incompleteness of rationality. Just as *In the Cage* touched explicitly on the possibility of evil, so Pythagoras will not allow a one-dimensional view of humanity but trails the possibility of magic as an enticement to follow and explore.

The outlandish apparatus of *Funland*, junk from heaven falling in a stream outside the window, priests and doctors who turn into crows and doves, has a weird appropriateness in the context of The Cedars. The other patients, particularly the three women whose dialogue is often rhythmical and chorus-like, are enclosed in their own obsessions. Kennedy, a visiting newspaperman, is enclosed in his own expectations and makes the significant error of mistaking the patient for the doctor. As he observes, to distinguish between the sane and insane would be useful, but it is not easy. Indeed, the psychiatrist confesses to his own obsessions and the superintendent is benignly obtuse. Pythagoras himself has, in Kennedy's words, the knack of delivering the 'searing truths of the insane.'

In this play also there are two finely managed set-pieces, the demonstration to students and the patients' concert, in which the rational and the irrational confront each other in a highly dramatic way, with thunder and lightning, collapses, coincidences, climaxes and anti-climaxes. There is always a 'normal' explanation available, but the stagecraft ensures that this would be a disappointment in theatrical terms, and the other dimension of magic and darkness becomes something we feel, as an audience, that we need. When the play ends, Pythagoras has reverted to simply Tony Smith, shorn of his powers and his mystery. Yet, as was the case with Mr Nott, the ambiguity is still there. For Mr Nott there is always tomorrow at the Sunshine Hall, for Pythagoras, the *possibility* that he can cause telephones to ring by pointing at them. The telephone bell is the last image of the play. Tony Smith is shaken—'I'll be all right in a sec.' The audience, like him, needs time to adjust. After a play so dense with suggestion, with echoes of Eliot in its language and wild improbabilities in its staging, the central enigma remains an enigma. Outside the theatre, rationality must remain sovereign, and coincidence must explain all; but within the world of the play we hope for something other, and welcome a power that seems to subvert the authority of the orthodox.

The conventions of the more ordinary kind of radio play, like those seen in *House of Cowards* with its near-cliché characters and non-specificity, have disappeared by the time we reach the later plays. But some of the characteristics of the best radio dramas remain, and *Pythagoras* had an especially fine production on Radio 3. Something of the play's visual impact was preserved, or rather transformed into aural terms, by the realisable context which was established as the broadcast progressed. The wild reminiscences of the patients, the jargon of the doctors and the bewildering fluency of Pythagoras intermingled in the sound equivalent of a light-show. And out of this swam the big questions.

There is, obviously, considerable variety amongst these plays. Their settings and situations range from the somewhat contrived to a *sui generis* inevitability, the characters from people we have met before in dramas to those who stand foursquare in their own being. In all the plays, though, in the characters, the action and the tone of the dialogue, there is a clear engagement with certain moral preoccupations; with the extent to which people are, or must be, aware of one another and therefore of obligations to one another; with a need, amounting to a duty, to reconcile the scientific attitude with the artist's vision; with the making of properly informed choices—informed, that is, with sympathy and understanding. In Dannie Abse's theatre, to be fully human is a responsible task.

1 Tales of Abse

D. J. ENRIGHT

Every picture tells a story, so why shouldn't poems? A story can be the 'objective correlative' which defines and vivifies the emotions and indeed the thoughts involved, concentrating the attention of both writer and reader, and saving the poet from the arbitrariness of 'mood' poems and the egotism of the disembodied *cri de coeur* or *cri de* whatever it is.

It is no bad thing for the verse writer to have some of the talents associated with the writer of fiction. Nor of course, if you look at the poetry of the past, is it a rare thing. The *Iliad, The Canterbury Tales, Paradise Lost, The Rape of the Lock, The Ancient Mariner.* . . True, these are long poems, even epics, but without trying very hard one can think of shorter story-poems or miniature dramas by George Herbert, Blake, Wordsworth ('We are Seven'), Browning, Hardy, Edward Thomas . . .

It seems to have been one of the effects of 'modernism,' with its animus against such verse narratives as *The Idylls of the King*, to give 'story' a bad name, and paradoxically to help to let loose on the literary world a flood of shapeless, unarticulated writing which—though its practitioners might have vague concepts of 'individualism' and 'self-expression' somewhere at the back of their minds—can only be seen as self-administered therapy of undetermined efficacy. Individualism is a sacred idea which I sometimes suspect doesn't really need all the protection we offer it. And as for self-expression, in the day-to-day story of living we mostly express ourselves in the course of dealings with *others*, other characters.

The advantages afforded by a 'story-line,' whether in the creation of a state of mind or in the depiction of a state of affairs, are evident in the poems of Dannie Abse. That a number of these are Jewish in theme is perhaps no reason for supposing story-telling to be a particularly Jewish trait, despite the tempting evidence of the Old Testament and, to take just one later example, the earthy spiritualities of Isaac Bashevis Singer, who recently complained that zeal for 'messages' has caused writers to forget to tell a tale. Quite a few writers of fiction have been Gentile, after all. Even so, we might look first at the Jewish stories and character sketches. Among them are 'Uncle Isidore,' that 'smelly schnorrer and lemon-tea bolshevik' borrowed from the pages of *Ash on a Young Man's Sleeve*, 'Snake' (the snake it was that died) and 'Of Rabbi Yose.' The last-named makes a sound rational point with more force than any abstract argument could summon up: the blind *are* more blind in the dark, because other people can't see them and hence fail to help them. In 'Of Itzig and his dog,' Itzig talks to God while out walking and God responds by making his dog's tail wag: which adds an amusing twist to the old and possibly Cabbalistic reversed-reading whereby God turns into man's best friend. Outstanding in this genre are the various 'Tales of Shatz': What has God been doing, a matron of Golders Green asks, since the Holy One appeared to her when she was a child? 'Waiting, waiting patiently, till you see Him again.'

Equally effective though often grimmer are the medical anecdotes, the best known of which must be 'In the theatre,' telling how during an operation for brain tumour a voice is heard to say 'leave . . . my . . . soul . . . alone . . .': it leaves the audiences at poetry readings not knowing whether to laugh or turn pale. The fairy-tales modernly medicalized in 'Pantomime diseases'—

> *Shy, in the surgery, red Riding Hood undressed*
> *—Dr Wolff, the fool, diagnosed Scarlet Fever*

—are playful rather than powerfully pointed or original, though it might be held that the author's being a doctor lends him more authority (or licence?) than would otherwise be the case. My own favourites in this line are the portrayal in 'The smile was' of the smiling Indian ('resigned, all the fatalism of the East') who declines to believe the doctor's assurance that he is well, and the fine terse poem 'Peachstone,' which is akin to some of D. H. Lawrence's most moving pieces:

I do not visit his grave. He is not there.
Out of hearing, out of reach. I miss him here,
seeing hair grease at the back of a chair
near a firegrate where his spit sizzled,
or noting, in the cut-glass bowl, a peach.

For that night his wife brought him a peach,
his favourite fruit,while the sick light glowed,
and his slack, dry mouth sucked, sucked, sucked,
with dying eyes closed—perhaps for her sake—
till bright as blood the peachstone showed

A third group consists of stories in which the writer himself features, though less as hero than as unhero or else mere bystander. 'The French master' is rather too plainly Audenesque in derivation, but 'The death of Aunt Alice'—

B., one night, fell screaming down a liftshaft.
'Poor fellow, he never had a head for heights'

—has proved a popular item in poetry readings, not surprisingly. A bright example of this genre is 'As I was saying': any self-respecting English-writing poet ought to know about wild flowers and their properties (cf. Wordsworth, John Clare, Edward Thomas), but this one doesn't—and isn't inclined to swot the subject up out of 'that W. H. Smith book.' Ignorance about 'Nature,' I am told, is a Jewish characteristic—because of those desert antecedents? Because why bother with the language of flowers when you have the language of God?—though I would have thought it a generalized urban characteristic. I have on my desk a Chatto Nature Guide to Wild Flowers, which I open dutifully from time to time, only to be baffled and repelled by language like 'the ovary is superior' or 'dense glandular-haired biennial to perennial, with dioecious red flowers' or (and this of Wordsworth's Lesser Celandine, mark you!) 'the plant is poisonous.'

If we are to continue in what Lawrence called the 'imitation-botanical fashion' of classifying literary works, we might assign to a separate category the stories not related but hinted at in passing. For instance, in 'One Sunday afternoon,' the reference to the squire who hanged himself 200 years before and 'according to the guidebook' became transparent. And indeed the girl spotted in the briefly stationary train in 'Not Adlestrop'—a poem which has less in common with the Edward Thomas it invokes than with Clough's 'Natura Naturans.' (Incidentally, Mrs Clough found the latter poem 'abhorrent' and excluded it from the posthumous collection of 1862 on the grounds that it was 'liable to great misconception.') Then there is a fine touch in the early 'Letter to *The Times*,' a comic-indignant anti-nature poem, when we are told that not only do the stars fail to warn us when they are about to fall but

> *They are even too lazy*
> *to shine when we are most awake.*

Lines like those, short short stories in themselves, can easily be missed.

Thereby hangs a tale, a sad story I must tell against myself. When a few years ago I was pasting up for an anthology that prime example of the story-poem, 'Florida,' itself another anti-nature poem, somehow or other the second stanza, containing the story within the story, went missing. How I shall never know. Reading and re-reading the poem in proof, I continually read the missing story as being there. Well, it is a good story—during the French Revolution the starving dowager served up Fido, her poodle, as a roast, remarking at the end of the meal,

> *What a damn shame Fido*
> *isn't alive to eat up all those nice*
> *crunchy bones left upon the plate*

—and I had heard the author read it, to great effect, many times. He wasn't entirely mollified, however, when I told him that why the stanza wasn't on the printed page was because it was imprinted on my brain. . .

2 Aspects of Narrative

BARBARA HARDY

Dannie Abse's short poems have a strong narrative inclination. Some poems are simple and straightforward acts of storytelling, some have a sufficient involution to propose an awareness of forms and language through narrative, others, especially in the recent volume, *Way Out in the Centre* (1981), make narrative serve a lyric purpose. In an introductory note to *Collected Poems, 1948–1976* (1977) Abse writes of a wish to create a resonant power of suggestions:

> For some time now my ambition has been to write poems which appear translucent but are in fact deceptions. I would have a reader enter them, be deceived he could see through them like sea-water, and be puzzled when he cannot quite touch bottom.

This is a new way of stating an old truth. Lessing spoke of the poet's creation of a 'pregnant moment,' Coleridge observed that poetry moves us most powerfully when least perfectly understood, and Yeats spoke of the need for restraint in passion, so that we feel 'the stirring of the beast beneath.' The need to enact rather than tell has become an important commonplace of modern criticism. But a poet may well describe aim rather than achievement, and Abse's use of narrative has not always freed itself from some excess and explicitness.

Abse's earliest poems (those he chose to re-publish in *Collected Poems*) engage us through a characteristic straightness and candour. Whether realistic slices-of-life or surrealistic fantasies, they tend often to take the reader from the surface to the depths with care and completeness. This solicitous guidance appears as a deliberated rhetorical emphasis, as in the poem 'The Uninvited.' Images of the uninvited powers are flickeringly invoked in glimpses and glances, 'light momentarily,' 'the weight of another world,' 'with flowers before the open door,' and 'the sunset pouring from their shoulders.' The imagery is not permitted to make its presence simply felt but is explicitly placed in a sequence of narrative, followed from a beginning (arrival) to the end (change). The story is also accompanied by explicit commentary which describes and explains effects: 'leaving us not so much / in darkness, but in a different place / and alone as never before.' The transparent statements of transformation take up nearly half the poem (ten lines out of twenty-one). Repetition is even underlined by being formalised in types of refrain, 'never before,' 'no longer,' 'ever.' The strength and mystery of visitation is weakened and solidified by the insistance on causality and interpretation. The poem seems to distrust the power of imagery, though that power is precisely what it needs (and even seems to wish) to invoke.

This combination of narrative sequence and completion forms the feeling in many poems. The poet's gift of fantasy is bestowed with one hand, tentatively, irrationally, vividly, and taken away with the other, anxiously, lucidly, rationally. The right hand knows only too well what the left hand is doing. Passion is sometimes dried up by reason. This happens not only in lyrical and imagistic poems like 'The univited,' but also in social and psychological sketches like 'Portrait of a marriage,' and in those allegorical poems which at times possess the sinister oddity and fantasy of Kafka or early Auden, but too often move away from irrational tones and terms into a rational discourse.

We may wish the ends of poems were absent, as in 'Albert' (*Collected Poems*) where symbol hardens into allegory in the last line, 'Albert hated dogs after, though this was absurd,' to lose initial mystery in an over-symmetrical and over-explanatory ending. A poem which begins with an inventive invocation is 'The second coming' (*Collected Poems*). Its surrealistic image presents the emergence of a mythological head from a strongly particularised sensuous earth. The story of the severed head joins old and new styles, but the poetry cannot let image and action speak for themselves, and ends with the imperative,

> *Dig, I say dig, you'll*
> *find arms, loins, white legs, to prove my story—*
> *and one red poppy in the corn.*

This is to weaken the symbolism with allegory. The significant detail about proving a story may be ironic but is redundant. This story doesn't need this proof. The process of narrative invention is a complex one and the poet doesn't seem always to trust his own telling. We are sometimes made to feel that we have touched bottom, and too easily.

There are, however, many exceptions in *Collected Poems*. The apparently open and simple poem about Agamemnon's sacrifice of Iphigenia, 'The Victim of Aulis,' eschews allegory, and allows idea to be embodied in sensation. In spite of the explicitness of topical suggestion, 'We have had nothing of education. / We must obey, being little men. / The cause is just,' there is the primary emotional and sensational impact of a calm, an influential event and an impassioned symbol. Generalisation is balanced by the particulars of sensation; the descriptions of the young girl are thoroughly imagined: 'and she trailing her small hands in the waters / playing with coloured beads of spray.' The poem has a repeated refrain of a tall slave singing: 'a tall slave sings— / sings of home and alien distances,' and at the end 'the tall slave sings why Father? why Father?' The poem curls in on itself, uses detail resonantly, to mark a sequence and an end. The climax is uttered quietly, and with a reflexive stroke which admits the pressure of time and tradition, and marks the fact of repeated fictionality.

Stories tend to be about stories, in different ways. 'The Victim of Aulis' reflects and reflects on fictionality briefly and implicitly, but many of the poems reflect more centrally and ambitiously. I do not refer to the many poems about the poet and the work, explicit poems like 'Public library' or allegorical ones like 'The magician' or 'The water diviner' or 'Red balloon,' but to more oblique treatments, like the meditation 'From a suburban window':

> *Such afternoon glooms, such clouds chimney low—*
> *London, the clouds want to move but can not,*
> *London, the clouds want to rain but can not—*
> *such negatives of a featureless day:*
> *the street empty but for a van passing,*
> *an afternoon smudged by old afternoons.*
> *Soon, despite railings, evening will come*
> *from a great distance trailing evenings.*
> *Meantime, unemployed sadness loiters here.*
>
> *Quite suddenly, six mourners appear:*
> *a couple together, then three stout men,*
> *then one more, lagging behind, bare-headed.*

Not one of the six looks up at the sky,
and not one of them touches the railings.
They walk on and on remembering days,
yet seem content. They employ the décor.
They use this grey inch of eternity,
and the afternoon, so praised, grows distinct.

Helen Vendler, in *Part of Nature, Part of Us*, reports that Robert
Lowell told a poetry class, a poem 'is an event, not the record of an
event.' The difference between 'The uninvited' or 'A second coming'
and this example of the poet at his most confidently implicit is
precisely the difference between record and event. The first half of
this poem refuses to narrate, sets up a scene, a climate, and an
emtion where the ordering of narration is inhibited. Every detail
insists on stasis, negation, idling, neutrality. The images assert a
lack of form, in time, space, and motion. With the second stanza,
the mood changes, to transform stasis into direction, vagueness into
precision. We move from idling into narrative energy and affective
occupation. Transformation of form and language is made explicit,
but in no complete or tautological way. The last two and a half lines
conclude the poem, but do not do the reader's work. We can only
assent to words like 'employ' and 'use' and 'grow distinct' if we
understand and interpret the work of structure and language, seeing
the poem itself become distinct by reminding us of the ordering
occupation of the act of mourning. The mourning is a remembering,
a praise, a ritual re-formation. Here we really enter a poem, to
experience the sensation of discovering depths dynamically. Meanings are not translated into discursive aids but proved intrinsically in
the poetic process.

In his most recent volume, *Way Out in the Centre*, even the most
simple story-poems have a nice subtlety. Itzig is one of the tellers of
tall tales who inhabit these poems, and 'Of Itzig and his dog'
presents his piety, cunning, and dottiness through the form of a
Shaggy Dog (or Shaggy God) story, using the traditional bathetic
climax to surprise us with the obvious and make a point about
narration in exposing the nature of outrageous and irrefutable faith:

When I say please God this
And thank God that,
Then God always makes, believe me,
The dog's tail wag.

Another poem in a similar vein is 'Snake,' which runs through interpretations and variants of a story about a snake who dies after biting a rabbi, ending with the cleanshaven Freudian rabbi who comes up with the obvious phallic story. The point is not just an amusing potted history but the impact of the modern incredible version on the amazed ancestral ghosts, 'handbones weighing moonshine.'

The narrative reflexiveness of these joke-poems can act as a model to define more complex writing, like 'Lunch and afterwards,' where Abse uses the device of narrative juxtaposition, this time for lyrical purposes. There is the story of science, a 'morbid verse of facts' recited by a pathologist:

> *'After death, of all soft tissues the brain's*
> *the first to vanish, the uterus the last.*

This is matched and capped by the poet's excursion into a fantasy about woman-eaters which registers horror, wonder, meeting the factuality of science with the affectivity of art:

> *'Yes,' I said, 'at dawn I've seen silhouettes*
> *hunched in a field against the skyline, each one*
> *feasting, preoccupied, silent as gas.*
>
> *Partial to women they've stripped women bare*
> *And left behind only the taboo food,*
> *The uterus, inside the skeleton.'*

The antithesis is sensitively blurred by the reminder at the end that the speakers are eating, as the first speaker picks meat from 'his canines,' observing 'You're a peculiar fellow, Abse.' The second half of the poem is sub-titled 'No reply,' and although its incantation registers hysterical force, it shows a lack of faith in the pressures of the first part. There seems to be no need to reply, no need to assert that the pathologist's words are unforgettable. The story of his story has said so. The interpretative activity of our response is inhibited.

A poem which has more faith in its images is the love poem 'Last Words'. It is about imagining the details of the ending, and proceeds through the recognition of fictions and the experience of truths. It poises the 'verbose deaths' of Shakespearean drama, and the biographical fictions of famous last words, against experience of actual death:

> *Most do not know who they are*
> *when they die or where they are, country or town,*
> *nor which hand on their brow*

Fictions and truths join in the speaker's last wish for last words:

> *And how would I wish to go?*
> *Not as in opera—that would offend—*
> *nor like a blue-eyed cowboy shot and short of words,*
> *but finger-tapping still our private morse, '. . . love you,'*
> *before the last flowers and flies descend.*

The poem dares to be wishful, but just avoids sentimentality by placing wishing in the context of actual life where wishes aren't horses to be ridden to brave deaths, and by putting the unspoken imagined last words before a last line whose last words remember the funeral ·flowers and the flies. The poem has insisted on the fictitious glories of fiction, as it composes its fiction to speak of the inseparable but unjoinable human twins of knowing and longing. 'Last Words' intelligently and feelingly reflects and reflects on facts about narrative, narrative representing the order and freedom of art. The prevailing feeling, in a special and personal meeting of doctor and poet, is an experienced and realistic compassion for certain human events.

Abse uses the doctor's experience as an effective type, sometimes an ideal, to bring emotional particularity to many narrative poems. The tension between two kinds of communication in one person's imagination is elegiacally moving in 'The doctor,' 'X-ray,' and in 'A winter visit' where the speaker, a son visiting his mother 'nearly ninety' moves between the free, outer world of the park and the enclosed, shrinking space inhabited by old age. He wants to bring messages, as one does, from the large world to the small, and after twists of rejection—the affirmative story of pale sperm's metamorphosis into peacock colours won't do—he brings an isolated and a communicable gift of image, 'four flamingoes / standing, one-legged on ice, heads beneath wings.' As in 'From a suburban window' the shaping of the narrated action corresponds with the shaping of response. The gift of image is made to the mother, in the poem, and to the reader, outside it. The teller of the story cannot bring her the affirmative telling, blending science and poetry, which he imagines, and the poem moves out of narrative into image, avoiding the linear sequence and conclusiveness, but in a way which creates a kind of ending. It dilates the sad story of a dying parent to the story of inhibited but inspired loving.

At his best, Abse not only analyses art, but does so with feeling and justified form. His sense of narrative ending is increasingly satisfying, reaching out instead of closing, and surprising instead of interpreting, moving on instead of back. Of the poems which move (in all senses of the word) by becoming gradually or suddenly opaque, I would praise 'The Power of Prayer' (which cheekily uses Herbert), 'Imitations,' 'Light,' 'Night Village,' 'The Empty Building at night' and 'Another street scene,' a powerful narrative poem which startles out of lucid communication to a frightening irrational refusal to narrate:

> *Truce! You have been led into fiction.*
> *Listen! Here comes a violin*
> *and tunes to make a donkey dance.*
>
> *The bearded man has closed his eyes.*
> *Who's this, disguised as a beggar,*
> *playing a violin without strings?*
>
> *What music's this, its cold measure?*
> *Who are these, dangling from lampposts,*
> *kicking as if under water?*

An ABC of Dannie Abse

JOHN ORMOND

White coat and purple coat
a sleeve from both he sews.
That white is always stained with blood
that purple by the rose.

And phantom rose and blood most real
compose a hybrid style;
white coat and purple coat
few men can reconcile.

White coat and purple coat
can each be worn in turn,
but in the white a man will freeze
and in the purple burn.

The words are those spoken by the character Pythagoras in Dannie Abse's play of the same name; his theme is the difficulty of wearing 'both the white coat of science and the magician's purple one.' The play received its first production in 1976 and confirmation that the two garbs derive from, and refer to, Dannie Abse's own experience as doctor and poet is provided in the section, 'Notes Mainly at The Clinic,' collected in his book, 'A Strong Dose of Myself,' published in 1983.

> . . . medicine has been for me, in some respects, a hobby
> that has been well paid, whereas poetry has been a central

activity paid poorly. I have worn a white coat so many hours a week and then, with relief, I have discarded it so that on enchanted or/and precarious occasions I could don a purple one. Or so it used to be. But over the years the white coat has gathered to itself a purple glint in some lights and the purple has assumed some white patches.

Re-reading Abse's poetry intensively I have been struck by the consistency of his timbre. By far the greater part of even the earliest work prefigures his later output, the voice and many of the themes and sources of imagery predicting modulations that were to come in his full maturity. If asked to choose just a single line to indicate the stance of the man in his dual world I would take from his poem 'Mysteries'

> . . . *a vision dies from being too long stared at*

which was collected in 1972; and would justify my choice by quoting from the collection that followed three years later. In this, in a poem entitled 'Remembrance Day,' Abse reiterates

> A *vision dies from being too long stared at.*

Here is a man of science who needs mysteries. The way in which the white coat has taken on a purple glint and the purple coat white patches can be recorded in an alphabetical arrangement of some of Dannie Abse's themes, imagery and concerns. The following is a mere indication of the complexity and the major achievement of this deeply human, and indeed vulnerable poet in that a key part of his knowledge is his sense of how little it is we know.

A

ADAM is the successor to the 'botched ANGELS' in 'Bedtime Story'; and father to the vagrants, down-and-outs, meths-drinkers and half-crazed unfortunates who sleep, with the rest of life's misfits, in their own excrement on park benches. But these, too, are men. See under SOHO and Z.

AFTERNOONS (LOST) The sight of very ordinary things can set a good poet off on a major theme. In 'Postmark' envelopes with official stamps make Abse think of death, Jewish funerals and lost afternoons. Such times of limbo often permeate his poems, as do the smells of quiet halls in suburban houses. So do dust in sunbeams, silent telephones and the silences after visitors have gone. The lost afternoons of 'Postmark' are the image that develops into a quiet and puzzled elegy.

ANGELS is a section in a triptych with ghosts and unicorns in a poem that is full of fun and typical of Abse's delight in a perverse notion when it pleases him. 'They own neither genitals nor public hair;' are redundant as artists' models; and 'Welsh hymns stampede their shadows entirely.' With that last observation I agree entirely.

APPLE In Eden, Eve munches and munches after her initial nibbling at the forbidden fruit. In his poem 'Transgression,' among his 'Jottings,' Abse seems to suggest that the sin was in going the whole hog, that if only she'd been less greedy God wouldn't have blown the whistle and sent her and her clubmate off the park. See under FOOTBALL.

ASTONISHMENT The everyday world presents Abse with a sufficiently complex set of stimuli for his vision. To have come upon lamplight burning in a brilliantly sunlit room will remain in his memory and become part of his metaphor (see MYSTERIES) for more unaccountable matters.

> *I start with the visible*
> *and am startled by the visible.*

B

BALLAD Abse is fond of the ballard form and often uses an early one, 'The Trial' in his public readings. See also the witty 'The Ballad of Oedipus Sex.'

BELIEF Looking for truth and using his art as a tool to that end Abse is rather like 'The Water Diviner' in his poem so titled. Searching, he says, in

> *Repeated desert, recurring drought,*
> *sometimes hearing water trickle,*
> *sometimes not, I, bu doubting first,*
> *believe; believing, doubt.*

110

See another early poem for its metaphor. 'The Mountaineers' ends: 'the more we climb the further we have to go.'

C

CABBALISTIC is not too far out as a word to give some impression of Dannie Abse's deliberately contrived effects. His basic good sense and his sense of the tight-rope he is on in 'Funland,' for example, keep him from pretentiousness, something he has guarded against since early on he shed the influence of Dylan Thomas—not that he ever really succumbed to it. Increasingly, over the years, Abse seems to have absorbed some of the manner of Hebrew poets. This can be seen by comparing his original work with his adaptations from Hebrew poems. Sometimes, as in 'Of Itzig and his dog,' it seems that he has been extending his range and enriching it by readings from ancient Jewish commentaries. e.g. from 'Of Rabbi Yose'

> *'Thou shalt grope at noonday*
> *as the blind gropeth in darkness.'*

See under THE TALMUD.

CANCER and its force of anti-life recurs, one way and another, in a number of works. Sometimes, as in 'Pathology of colours,' the medical practitioner's eye is present:

> *I know the colour rose, and it is lovely,*
> *but not when it ripens in a tumour;*

while at others, Abse uses the doctor's special position for observation. His 'In the theatre' puts into service a terrifying story, related to him by his brother Dr Wilfred Abse, of a brain operation that went badly wrong. This poem is a dark and frightening thing and chills audiences when Dannie Abse reads it in public after giving reassurances that the kind of operation described was performed in a very different era of surgery.

Abse can also use medical material with wit and mischief, as in a *divertissement* entitled 'Pantomime diseases,' a piece that Robert Graves would call a 'left-handed poem':

> *Snow White suffered from profound anaemia.*
> *The genie warned, 'Aladdin you'll go blind,'*

111

when that little lad gleefully rubbed his lamp.
The Babes in the Wood died of pneumonia.
D. Whittington turned back because of cramp.

But in general when it comes to illnesses they are death-bringing. E.g. 'The Silence of Tudor Evans,' 'The case' and others. See under FATHER and MOTHER.

Cardiff Dannie Abse's home city, celebrated, as the background to his youth and as a place to which he has always returned, in many pieces. Vividly evoked in various poems like 'The game':

> *Saturday afternoon has come to Ninian Park*
> *and, beyond the goal posts, in the Canton Stand*
> *between black spaces, a hundred matches spark.*

And in 'Return to Cardiff,' scene of 'my first botched love affair,' (cf 'botched angels' above) where for all his returnings, and his unendingly ardent and often incomprehensible loyalty to Cardiff City AFC's 'Bluebirds,' Abse has sometimes found it a place

> *where the boy I was not and the man I am not*
> *met, hesitated, left double footsteps, then walked on.*

Cardiff is also the setting for certain poems about people remembered, as in 'The French master': (Walter Bird, known as Wazo . . . his eyes the colour of a poison bottle').

CELEBRATION, POEM OF A poem first collected in *Tenants of the House* which shows Abse demonstrating the early intonations of his mature voice and making statements which are in musical and intellectual accord with poetry written in his late fifties:

> *The noise divides from the light.*
> *Bold astronomers who at night*
> *peep through the window-pane of the colossal skies*
> *look too far for the furthest star.*
> *This world confirms my senses.*

In the poem 'Anniversary' that precedes 'Poem of celebration' in Abse's arrangement of his *Collected Poems* the last two lines show him sharply aware that the world confirmed by his senses must be celebrated while we can:

> My dear, my dear, what perishes?
> I hear this voice in a voice to come.

Meanwhile

> I'll say 'I will' and 'I can'
> and like an accident breathe in space and air.

CHARM Abse shows in all sorts of ways, not least by his ability to see himself as the vulnerable man he is, as we all are. Dannie Abse is able to laugh at himself: as when he finds himself getting up at night, sleepless, and counting the Christmas cards about the room. Or he makes, in his poem 'A New Diary', a litany of the names of the old London telephone exchanges and of girls' names and feigns panic that the girls will not remember him.

> This clerk-work, this first January chore
> of who's in who's out. A list to think about
> when absences seem to shout, Scandal! Outrage!
> So turning to the blank, prefatory page
> I transfer most of the names and phone tags
> from last year's diary. True, Meadway, Speedwell,
> Mountview, are computer-changed into numbers,
> and already their pretty names begin to fade
> like Morwenna, Julie, Don't-Forget-Me-Kate,
> grassy summer girls I once swore love to.
> These, whispering others and time will date.
>
> Cancelled, too, a couple someone else betrayed,
> one man dying, another mind in rags.
> And remembering them my clerk-work flags,
> bitterly flags, for all lose, no-one wins,
> those in, those out, this at the heart of things.
> So I stop, ask: whom should I commemorate,
> and who, perhaps, is crossing out my name now
> from some future diary? Oh my God,
> Morwenna, Julie, don't forget me, Kate.

D

DARKNESS Images of darkness abound, in night streets, in uncurtained windows at night, as in 'Hunt the Thimble':

> *The brooding darkness then,*
> *that breeds inside a cathedral*
> *of a provincial town in Spain*

and darkness that come from lift-shafts; and the darkness inside a dead man's mouth. Even in 'Sunsets'

> *Darkness, like terror, lies within the scene.*
> *Music of Mozart merely seems serene.*

But that does not mean an acceptance:

> *Sunsets only exist that I may write*
> *about them; yet I'd dip my pen in light.*

DECEPTION An extract from Abse's introduction to his 'Collected Poems':

> For some time now my ambition has been to write poems which appear translucent but are in fact deceptions. I would have a reader enter them, be deceived he could see through them like sea-water, and be puzzled when he can not quite touch bottom.

I am reminded of something that Robert Graves told me of how he replied when the young Dylan Thomas sent him poems, asking for advice: 'They are too damned professional. . . He remained a professional,' Graves continued, 'but concealed it by firing deliberately off target.'

DOMESTICITY The delightful vignette 'Not Adlestrop' with its wink of affection for Edward Thomas's poem sees Abse at a train window in a station gazing at a girl on the platform:

> *When I, all instinct,*
> *stared at her, she, all instinct, inclined her head away*
> *as if she'd divined the much married life in me.*

After 'A night out' at the cinema and seeing a film depicting the horrors of a concentration camp the comforts of love and the solaces of the flesh are needed:

> *together we climbed the stairs,*
> *undressed together, and naked together,*
> *in the dark, in the marital bed, made love.*

DUALITY The early poem of that title begins

> *Twice upon a time,*
> *there was a man who had two faces*

and Abse sustains the conceit of doubles throughout the piece until he calls quits. It's a device of imagery he is very fond of. It crops up like a thumbprint. In 'The young man and the lion':

> *The lion wanted only that man .*
> *whose double tears it had drunk.*

And in 'Lunch and afterwards' when the poet has learned from a pathologist that

> *'After death, of all soft tissue the brain's*
> *the first to vanish, the uterus the last'*

back home

> *because I shan't forget that ever*
> *because I walked into the hall where*
> *I stood next to the telephone*
> *I thought of a number doubled it.*

Of course, the last line derives from the schoolboy arithmetical trick. Think of a number. Double it. Add (say) 10. Half it. Take away the number you first thought of. The answer is always half the number you added on, so here it is 5. It's a futile trick, telling one nothing. And the futile new piece of information that the poet's brain now contains, that the brain decays first after death, tells him nothing that can make life and death more comprehensible. To double the telephone number is an act of defiance against the darkness of the world.

E

EMPTINESS The poet passes the dark vacancy of the unoccupied skyscraper on his way home:

> *I would ignore the dark building devoid of men*
> *and deny again that the emptiness inside it*
> *is part of my life. . .*

ENDURANCE The poem 'The motto' ends with an italicised line which could serve as an instruction to all men looking for revelations in a world where none are really likely to materialise; in which the poet, especially, must try to play a waiting game:

> *Be visited, expect nothing, and endure.*

EPITHALAMION A lovely lyric from Abse's earliest book:

> *Shipwrecked, the sun sinks down harbours*
> *of a sky, unloads its liquid cargoes*
> *of marigolds . . .*

The fine verbal thrust is that of a young poet, but the poem's end brings acknowledgement that for all the delights and luxuriances of love

> *today I took to my human bed*
> *flower and bird and wind and world,*
> *and all the living and all the dead.*

As The Talmud says, 'The world is a wedding.' See under THE TALMUD.

ESSENCE The scene could be the large lawn inside Cardiff Castle. With his aged mother during 'A winter visit,' the loving, caring and medically-qualified son walks slowly with her as the peacocks screech. Her life is nearly ended.

116

Dare I affirm to her, so aged and so frail,
that from one pale dot of peacock's sperm
spring forth all the colours of a peacock's tail?

I do. But she like the sibyl says, 'I would die';
then complains, 'This winter I'm half dead, son.'
And because it's true I want to cry.

F

FAMILY In poems like 'Cousin Sidney' and 'The Death of Aunt Alice' Abse presents convincing potrayals of characters and circumstances. The first of these poems is so haunting and the second so funny that it does not matter, to me at least, whether or not the characters are true or invented. They have all the ring of the authentic, but rise above the merely personal:

> *Aunt crying and raw in the onion air*
> *of the garden (the unswinging empty swing);*

and the doom-tongued Aunt Alice's funeral going off without a single hitch, which she would have hated

> *For alive you relished high catastrophe*
> *your bible Page One of a newspaper.*

See, similarly UNCLE ISODORE.

FATHER There is a deep sadness in Abse's poems about his father, of course, but it is a sadness that is more than simply filial. As he is dying 'In Llandough Hospital', just outside Cardiff, the son says

> *'To hasten night would be humane,'*
> *I, a doctor, beg a doctor,*
> *for still the darkness will not come—*
> *his sunset slow, his first star pain.*

The death, the personal world of grief, serve but to make the cosmic riddle even more insoluble. Being a doctor has not helped; it has somehow laid bare, because of his helplessness, a greater vulnerability.

> *so like a child I question why*
> *night with stars, then night without end.*

Later something approaching anger flares after an 'Interview with a spirit healer.'

> *I loathe his trade,*
> *the disease and the sanctimonious lie*
> *that cannot cure the disease. My need,*
> *being healthy, is not faith; but to curse the day*
> *I became mortal the night my father died.*

See also 'Peachstone,' and the use of 'my father' in the poem 'Bedtime story,' seemingly simple and about origins and ends at first, but then develops with the themes of judgement and possibility.

FOOTBALL See CARDIFF, and also how Abse uses the sound of a football bouncing in 'One Sunday afternoon' to give him initially a sense of isolation but later one of comfort. See also an early poem 'The game':

> *The coin is spun. Here all is simplified,*
> *and we are partisan who cheer the Good,*
> *hiss at passing Evil. Was Lucifer offside?*
> *A wing falls down when cherubs howl for blood.*
> *Demons have agents: the Referee is bribed.*

FORM Defined by Abse (in 'After a departure') as 'decorative logic.' Cf. C. M. Bowra: 'A poet must take care to choose a form which enables him to say exactly what he means in all its range and its subtlety.'

G

God See 'Sunsets':

> *Mystics to keep awake close their eyes,*
> *and in eternal emptiness, feel wise.*
> *God is what that great nothing signifies.*

GOLDERS GREEN an area in North London where Dannie Abse has had his home for many years. Apart from one collection of his poems which was called *Poems, Golders Green* its significance to Abse is that the passers-by and the general ebb and flow of shoppers remind him of his Jewishness since it is an area where many Jews have chosen to live. It is also a symbol of suburbia. See 'Here,' 'Another street scene,' and many others with imagery drawn from gardens, night streets and so on.

GOSSIP From the marvellous poem 'Mysteries,' which I regard as a kind of Rosetta Stone to the various languages inside Abse's whole work, I point to

> *I should know by now that few octaves can be heard,*
> *that a vision dies from being too long stared at;*
>
> *that the whole of recorded history even*
> *is but a little gossip in a great silence. . .*

H

HALLS Front halls, places of the receiving of visitors, of news arriving in letters.

> *Halls of houses own a sweet biscuity smell;*
> *and the carpet's frayed, the staircase lonely.*

'Halls' is a poem obsessive about halls: places where telephones ring, sometimes unanswered. As 'At the Tate' Gallery, they will often have

> *parquet floors,*
> *as Rodin's lovers keep on kissing*
> *and not kissing.*

Unreal, as a stage set is unreal, when, in the domestic halls

> *guests leaving, slightly drunk, deranged,*
> *know neither the hall nor the host, smileless.*

Yes, 'Arcane, unparaphrasable halls.'
See 'Postmark'.

HINTS What are things trying to tell us? What tidings, and of what sort, are about to come?

> *Unfocused voices in the wind, associations, clues,*
> *odds and ends, fringes caught, as when, after the doctor quit,*
> *a door opened and I glimpsed the white enormous face*
> *of my grandfather, suddenly aghast with certain news.*

The time recalled turns out to be 'smoke in the memory' in a 'city of strangers, alien and bleak,' in Abse's 'Return to Cardiff.'

HOSPITAL See under FATHER and MOTHER.

HUMOUR Many examples, an excellent one being 'Miss Book World' in which a literary bunch of judges all potential lay-abouts eye the contestants for the title as

> *a harem for us;*
> *not that they are, but we imagine them so,*

> *The illusion over, half the contestants*
> *still fancy themselves in their knock-out pose,*
> *while we literati return to the real*
> *world of fancy, great poetry and prose;*
> *not that it is, but we imagine it so,*
> *great vacant visions in which we delight,*
> *as if we see the stars not only at night.*

I

IDENTITIES See under CARDIFF

> *where the boy I was not and the man I am not*
> *met, hesitated, left double footsteps, then walked on.*

For

> The return journey to Cardiff seemed less a return than a raid on mislaid identitites. . .

See also, above, the references to the white coat and the purple coat.

INVISIBLE 'I feel sometimes,' says Abse in the introduction to his play *Pythagoras* 'that the earth is no ordinary hosptial but a lunatic asylum whose inmates live out suffering lives of black comedy.' From the protagonist of the play, 'The Magician,' who increasingly attracts the poet's interest, there come these words:

> Normally a man in a factory thinks of his domestic problems, is preoccupied. He does not hear the clanging of metal all about him nor the buzz of a bluebottle on a lathe. But if he opened his soul as mine is open then he'd hear everything. He'd hear the harmony of the spheres and he'd see the invisible.

And a moment later he is saying, 'To really believe, people like you must doubt first.' Another character in the play, a doctor, remarks, '. . . we all have powers which we do not generally call upon, powers which we hardly know we own.' Pythagoras adds, '. . . like thinking I could make that phone ring.' He points to it. It rings.

J

JEW Like Dannie Abse, I happen to be Welsh, so we are fellow-countrymen; and he is also a Jew which I am not. While he has always shown himself conscious of his additional heritage there is evidence that, if anything, in more recent years he has if not actually grown *more* conscious of it then at least he has used, more directly and consistently, a greater leavening of Jewish material and allusion in his poems.

It would have been unnatural for him not to have been affected and moved by his first visit to Israel to give poetry-readings. But whether or not this stimulated him to greater application to readings from the Jewish commentaries, I cannot say. Certainly later poems such as 'Of Rabbi Yose,' with its wisdoms, derives from ancient discussions and wisdoms of the Jewish people. But the 'Song for Dov Shamir' (an 'invented' Israeli poet, the invention fooled T. S. Eliot) shows that Abse knew the location of both his sets of roots from the beginning. It could scarcely have been otherwise.

I did not know Dannie Abse's father but it was my privilege to be acquainted with his aged mother in her last years (we lived in adjacent streets in Cardiff). We found we had a great deal to talk about in that I knew the small town of Ystalyfera in the Swansea

Valley where she was born and where, in turn, her mother had spoken Welsh—

> *Welsh*
> *with such an accent the village said, 'Tell the truth, fach,*
> *you're no Jewess. They're from the Bible. You're from Patagonia!'*

This and the following from 'Car journey.'

> *I'm driving down the M4 again under bridges that leap*
> *over me then shrink in my side mirror. Ystalyfera is farther*
> *than smoke and God further than all distance known. I whistle*
> *no hymn but an old Yiddish tune my mother knows. It won't keep.*

But what *does* keep is the assault of a 'too lifelike Polish film about a concentration camp in Hitler's Germany . . . I quit that cinema in an undefined rage.' Hardly undefined, since it is written in the blue tattoo numbers of his race. The direct result, the poem 'A night out.' And what *does* keep, too, is the insomnia suffered in a German hotel:

> *The streets of Germany are clean*
> *Like the hands of Lady Macbeth. . .*
>
> *the wind seeps through a deep*
> *frost hole that is somewhere else*
> *carrying the far Jew-sounds of railway trucks.*

But Abse cannot be orthodox:

> *All God's robots lose their charm*
> *who carry prayer books, wear a hat.*
> *I don't like them, I don't like them,*
> *and feel less guilty thinking that.*

JOAN Joan Abse (née Mercer), married to Dannie Abse since 1951. Author, notably of the acclaimed biography *John Ruskin: The Passionate Moralist*. Studied art history at the Courtauld Institute. Dedicatee, with their three children, of the *Collected Poems* and of the ensuing collection *Way Out in the Centre*. See DOMESTICITY above.

122

K

KNOWLEDGE See again 'Mysteries':

> *. . . the whole of recorded history even*
> *is but a little gossip in a great silence.*

L

LIGHT and LIGHTS are recurring images too frequent to chronicle: sodium lamp-posts 'hosing empty roads with gold'; Soho lights of brothels, clubs and pubs; 'Lights in the night suburb,' where people peer out of their windows; orange belisha beacons blinking at 3 a.m. for no one. There's a theatrical quality in the way Dannie Abse uses lighting effects. By this I do not mean stagey.

LONDON See under GOLDERS GREEN and SOHO.

M

MAGIC Abse's delight on occasion in a kind of verbal flourish, almost a sleight of hand with words, shuffling now from the top now from the bottom of his vocabulary, is seen in 'The Magician.' Similarly it is a perfect example of the poet as stage-lighting manager:

> *Transformed by glamorous paraphernalia—*
> *tall top hat, made-up face, four smoking spotlights—*
> *only fellow magicians can sense beneath*
> *that glossy surface, a human failure.*

More is meant than an Archie Rice-type illusionist manqué.

Perhaps the poem is the first germ of the long poem *Funland* and of the play *Pythagoras*. In the preface to the play Abse writes: 'I was becoming more and more interested in the personality of those who are thought by others, rightly or wrongly, to own peculiar, even mysterious powers.'

MEDICINE 'The Smile Was' is a poem springing directly from medical experience, the smile being that of a mother who has newly given birth; the purity and timelessness of the smile is contrasted with those of others including that of a surgeon who 'draws a ritual wound / a calculated wound / to heal. . . ,' and whose 'secretive' smile is concealed behind a surgical mask. The surgeon's smile is 'luxuriant as the smile of Peter Lorre,'—that blandly-smug, oily and generally seedy smiler of so many good crime films, notably John Huston's 'The Maltese Falcon.' Although the poem demonstrates that Dannie Abse is not afraid of taking risks (he chides Leonardo da Vinci for only making 'Mona Lisa look six months gone,' there are near-banalities:

> But the smile, the smile
> of a new mother,
> what
>   an extraordinary
>   open thing
>   it is.

Related to 'The smile was' is the poem which Abse places at the end of his *Collected Poems 1949–1976*. This, 'The stethoscope,' is a complete triumph.

> Through it,
> over young women's abdomens tense,
> I have heard the sound of creation
> and, in a dead man's chest, the silence
> before creation began.

To quote from it at all is to run the danger of maiming it, for it is a complete thing. To praise the instrument would be to

> praise speech at midnight
> when men become philosophers

and to hear

> night cries
> of injured creatures, wide-eyed or blind;
> moonlight sonatas on a needle;
> lovers with doves in their throats; the wind
> travelling from where it began.

MIRACLES

> I said, every day, you can see
> conjunctions equally odd—awake and sane, that is—
> a tangerine on the snow, say.
> Such things are no more incredible than God.

MISFITS See SOHO but note also in 'Car journeys' when in the middle of nowhere at night

> fabulous in the ghastly wash
> of headlights, a naked man approached
> crying without inhibition, one hand to his face,
> his somehow familiar mouth agape.

> This road to Paradise, I muttered.

MOTHER Apart from the various references mentioned already ('Car journeys: Down the M4' and 'A winter visit'), compare 'In Llandough Hospital' with the poem 'X-ray.' The poet has just referred to the ineptitude of his hands when he was a boy.

> And this larger hand's the same. It stretches now
> out from a white sleeve to hold up, mother,
> your X-ray to the glowing screen. My eyes look
> but don't want to; I still don't want to know.

There is no purple upon the white sleeve. I have never heard Dannie Abse deliver the poems about his parents at any of his public readings.

MYSTERIES Mysteries are insoluble, cannot be ignored and are, in fact, needed.

'I should know by now that few octaves can be heard' Abse says in the poem 'Mysteries,' and returns to the keyboard in the poem that is at once dedication and epigraph to the collection *Way Out in the Centre* there to insist that what we hear of the truth in the face of mysteries must be rejoiced in:

> one note's gone from the piano
> —the highest. Listen to the thud of felt.

125

No, dear, no! Hear rather the other notes
of the right hand. Also the left background.
Their rejoicing, lamenting, candid sound.

But Abse also deliberately constructs mysteries, the best example
of this perhaps 'In the gallery,' a poem of which he gives a fascinating technical account in the section 'On rhyming and not rhyming'
in 'A Strong Dose of Myself.' The poems ends in a manner that
would have delighted Wallace Stevens, although Stevens is a poet
for whom Abse can muster no real passion, and the echo is therefore
unwitting.

Outside it is snow snow
snowing and namelessness is growing.

Yesterday four hoofmarks in the snows
rose and flew away.

They must have been four crows.
Or, maybe, three of them were crows.

Similarly, in 'Here' (another Golders Green poem) see the unaccountable appearance one afternoon of a ribboned horse and cart, the
driver in top hat, with a load of inflated balloons:

still I savour
its bland mystery, the oddness of it,
the unfathomable, blind, rare uses
I may make of it . . .

'Watching a cloud' he asks, 'Let me believe in angels for an hour.'
The need for something in the vacuum of belief, 'the thirst that from
the soul doth rise,' is unassuageable. We are always on the haunted
brink of what might be revealed, and

There are moments when a man must praise
the astonishment of being alive,
when small mirrors of reality blaze
into miracles; and there's One always
who, by never departing, almost arrives.

126

N

NAMELESSNESS Two related poems: 'The nameless' and 'The case,' the first a dark piece of dread of the blankness of death,

> *the abyss*
> *below everything, a hole in the eye,*
> *a hole in the earth, a hole in the memory.*

(Cf. David Gascoyne's 'Inferno' on 'the Void that undermines the world' with its 'bottomless depths of roaring emptiness.')

The second poem, 'The case' takes for theme a doctor colleague who knows the condition of one of his patients in hospital but not the man's name. Dr Abse is there to give a second opinion:

> *'Good morning, John,' I said,*
> *reading his name from the temperature chart.*

Dannie Abse once told me of the way in which he sometimes reassures nervous patients when they come back for a check-up after a lengthy period. 'How's your mother's sciatica?' he'll ask, or 'Did the dog get better?' And they reply, 'Fancy you remembering *that*, doctor, what a memory you've got.' The good doctor had merely noted bits of the previous year's outpourings on their record cards.

NIGHT See LIGHT but also '3 a.m. in the High Street' for night as a symbol of darkness beyond:

> *I think Virgil could take me by the hand*
> *past this butcher's shop, and show me, on the hooks,*
> *two live heads, one gnawing at the other.*
>
> *Look how that god, for Time's sake, unappeased,*
> *contemplates through its yellow monocle*
> *all that it now owns, blankly hating it.*

Part of the same namelessness and blankness and middle-of-the-night dread is in 'Nothing':

> *In sleep, dreams between long blanks;*
> *awake, blanks between brief dreams.*

This is the cemetery side of 50.
This is the taste of pure water.
This is the dread revealing nothing.

O

OMENS Remembering that Dannie Abse is 'startled by the visible' and knowing his awareness of

> *the irreducible strangeness of things*
> *and the random purposes of dreams*

it is not surprising that his unconscious mind sometimes rearranges the visible and creates sounds to accompany the new juxtapositions. In 'The weeping' the effect is ominous:

> *Not the most woeful sound a man may hear,*
> *an exile weeping and weeping.*
> *Yet desolate it is*
> *like a ram's horn blown*
> *in a hushed synagogue,*
> *like Christian bells opening, closing,*
> *like the muezzin heard*
> *even after he has ceased.*

P

PARADOX Sometimes used for effect as, indeed, in the opening lines of 'The weeping,' just mentioned:

> *After I lean from my shadow*
> *to switch on the dark in the lamp.*

But used, too, gnomically, and to me more satisfyingly in a poem like 'Sunsets':

The distance between two stars is night.
I stare and stare at dark till dark is bright.
Must I first go blind to have second sight?

Dannie Abse has always been fond of the device. An earlier poem 'The race' ends

> Ahead I see the winning post.
> I finish first and so have lost
> and speed into my walking ghost.

And consider the titles of some of his books of poems: *A Small Desperation; Way Out in the Centre.*

POET After a poetry reading, clearly feeling slightly short-changed by the urban settings of the poems she has heard, a lady asks Dannie Abse why it is that he does not write poems about the countryside, or at least work in the odd wild flower or two. The poem 'As I was saying' is his reply:

> I'll not compete with those nature poets you advance,
> some in country dialect, and some in dialogue
> with the country—few as calm as their words:
> Wordsworth, Barnes, sad John Clare who ate grass.

PYTHAGORAS Name of one of the patients featured in the long, disturbing but sometimes funny surrealistic poem *Funland* which is set in a mental home. The purple cloak is glimpsed again—this time that of the wizard, Merlin.

> Nobody else sees it (near the thornbush)
> the coffin rising out of the ground
> the old smelly magician himself no less
> rising out of the coffin.
>
> He gathers about him his mothy purple cloak.

Because of its surrealistic approach, I for one cannot be absolutely sure that I am getting the whole effect of what the poet intended. Pythagoras founds a Society in the asylum; and it was one of the teachings of the Pythagorean Brotherhood in Croton, as part of the doctrine of dualism, that every soul, involved in the conflict of good and evil, wants to escape from its endless cycle of lives and deaths and searches for rest. *Funland* ends

129

Do not wake us. We may die.

The echo of the last line of 'The Love Song of J. Alfred Prufrock' is deliberate:

Till human voices wake us, and we drown.

In the introduction to his play *Pythagoras* Dannie Abse says, having quoted Eliot's lines

The whole world is our hospital
Endowed by the ruined millionaire,

that he feels 'Sometimes . . . that the earth is no ordinary hospital but a lunatic asylum whose inmates live out suffering lives of black comedy.'

Q

QUESTION After his lunch with the pathologist who has imparted the information that 'After death, of all soft tissues the brain's / the first to vanish, the uterus the last,' the poet goes home to an empty house. The poem 'No reply' opens with the single word 'Why?' and continues with a long incantatory list of reasons:

because I'm Welsh because I'm a Jew
because the audible clock's rounder
than any circle I can draw
because I've shared the particular
lunatic boredom of caged animals
because I've been touched on a scar
and felt nothing or almost nothing . . .

Then he goes into the hall, thinks of a telephone number, and doubles it; an existentialist act. See under DUALITY.

R

RIDDLES 'Being a religious man Shatz adored riddles.' Not far from Dannie Abse's own position in that he needs mysteries.

Perhaps it is not possible to be an artist without religious inclination, no matter how seemingly non-practising.

ROMANTICISM Dannie Abse has moved away from the Neo-Romantic effect of his early work. But traces are left in the *Collected Poems*, as in the ending of 'The second coming.' The scene is a cornfield:

> *—and now that noble head is gone,*
> *a liquid redness in the yellow*
> *where the mouth had been.*
>
> *Dig, I say, dig, you'll*
> *find arms, loins, white legs, to prove my story—*
> *and one red poppy in the corn.*

S

SEXUALITY The early, very lovely poem 'Two voices,' in formal stanzas, Yeatsian in inflexion, indicates Dannie Abse's lyric reserves which he has been careful against using to excess:

> *I'll be all things you would be,*
> *the four winds and the seven seas,*
> *you'll play with such a gaiety*
> *devastating melodies*
> *till music be my body.*

SOHO The clinic in which Dr Abse has worked for many years is near the Soho area of London, and the district has given him various images, and has accorded him some of his basic themes. He sees

> *Three street musicians in mourning overcoats*
> *worn too long, shake money boxes this morning,*
> *then afterwards, play their suicide notes.*

The poem ends,

> *'Suddenly, there are too many ghosts about.'*

A more powerful poem, 'The Test' (the T of Test, unusually, in upper-case), is set in Soho Square with its statue of Charles II; it is a summer lunchtime,

> *mild clerks and secretaries carnival the grass.*

The poet is accosted by a seedy woman alcoholic. Empty and despairing, helpless and guilty, as this figure rants away

> *. . . I, fastidious as any office man,*
> *though licensed friend to Caliban, turn away,*
> *turn from her stridency in slow sorrow and distate.*

SOCCER See under CARDIFF

T

THE TALMUD It seems that, increasingly Dannie Abse has turned to the teachings and legends of The Talmud and other Jewish sources for solace and for starting-points for poems. See, for example, 'Another street scene'; and, especially, 'Of Rabbi Yose':

> *'Neighbour,' he cried, 'why this torch*
> *since you are blind?' The night waited*
> *for an answer: the wind in a carob tree,*
> *two men, one blind, both bearded, so many*
> *shadows thrown and fleeing from the torch.*

> *'So that others may see me, of course,'*
> *replied the neighbour, 'and save me*
> *from quicksand and rock. . .'*

U

UNCLE ISADORE The figure in the poem of that name who, 'fitting the violin to his beard' asks

> *'What difference between*
> *the silence of God and the silence of men?'*

His death is near and, like his life and many another,

> *he played and he played not to that small child*
> *who, big-eyed, listened—but to the Master*
> *of the Universe, blessed be his name.*

132

THE UNINVITED Title of a moving, although ambiguous, poem which prefaces the *Collected Poems 1948–1976*. Perhaps about the making of poems. It does not matter.

> *They came into our lives unasked for.*
> *There was light momentarily, a flicker of wings,*
> *a dance, a voice, and then they went out*
> *again, like a light, leaving us not so much*
> *in darkness, but in a different place*
> *and alone as never before.*
>
> *So we have been changed*
> *and our vision no longer what it was,*
> *and our hopes no longer what they were;*
> *so a piece of us has gone out with them also,*
> *a cold dream subtracted without malice,*
>
> *the weight of another world added also,*
> *and we did not ask, we did not ask ever*
> *for those who stood smiling*
> *and with flowers before the open door.*
>
> *We did not beckon them in, they came in uninvited,*
> *the sunset pouring from their shoulders,*
> *so they walked through us as they would through water,*
> *and we are here, in a different place,*
> *changed and incredibly alone,*
> *and we did not know, we do not know ever.*

V

VISION See the introduction: 'A vision dies from being too long stared at' and reference to 'I am startled by the visible.'

VOCABULARY For all the seeming directness of Dannie Abse's most usual manner, his vocabulary can have one (or, at least, me) reaching for the best dictionary to hand. Three examples: 'Our eidetic visions blur,' 'theurgic vapour trails,' and 'dybbuk' which I had to track down in Leo Rosten's *The Joys of Yiddish*. But one always finds that such words have been very precisely used.

W

WIT abounds. An early example, 'Letter to *The Times* 'beginning with a worked-up tirade against roses:

> *When they are ripped*
> *from the earth expiring, we sigh for them,*
> *prescribe tap-water, aspirin, and salt.*
>
> *But when we lie down under the same earth,*
> *in a dry silly box, do they revive us?*

X

X-RAY See under MOTHER

Y

YEATS To the early, self-acknowledged influences, those of Dylan Thomas and Rilke, I think I would suspect, at least in stanza forms, that of Yeats. See 'New Babylons':

> *Oppose, oppose, orthodoxies.*
> *Though the furnace doors are shut,*
> *small fires leap up high.*
> *Cornet, drum, and sackbut,*
> *could raise a tyrant's melodies*
> *and the severe Judges cry:*
> *'Conform, conform or die.'*

Z

Z Back to the beginning, the notion of Alpha and Omega. The botched angels, the men before and after Adam, the misfits, the meths drinkers and the street musicians playing 'their suicide notes' could have among their number, for all their flawed lineage, one who may be seen, albeit briefly,

sometimes in the last light of January,
in treeless districts of cities, in a withered
backstreet, their leader can be glimpsed from trains.

He stands motionless in long black overcoat
on spoilt snow and seems like a man again
who yet, father, will outlast the letter Z.

A Grateful Letter to Dannie Abse

DONALD DAVIE

Dear Dannie,
I have never thanked you properly for your response, a couple of
years ago, to an overture from some of my surrogate children, students in Tennessee. You responded by sending them, for a collection
they were making of small 'tributes' to me, a remarkable poem.
Since then you have paid me the further compliment of taking a
phrase from this poem—'Way Out in the Centre'—for the title of a
collection of your poems. This seems to mean that you set much
store by this poem, as I do also. And because I'm proud of having
provoked the poem, or at least occasioned it, I shall give myself the
pleasure of writing it out:

A Note to Donald Davie in Tennessee

Wigged gluttony never your style but will you
            always eschew,
barbered, the anorexia of fanaticism?
Though we would seldom sign the same petition
or join awkwardly the same shouting march,
neither of us, I hope, would leave through those doors
on the right or the left marked HYGIENE.

Donald, you're such a northern-rooted man
            you've moved again.
Is home only home away from it? Still poets
jog eagerly, each molehill mistaken

136

for Parnassus—such energy articulate!
But where's the avant-garde when the procession
runs continually in a closed circle?

So many open questions to one who prefers
        fugitive ways.
Of course I salute your gifted contradictions—
your two profiles almost the same—like Martin Guerre's.
I too am a reluctant puritan, feel uneasy
sometimes as if I travelled without ticket.
Yet here I am in England way out in the centre.

It will always be the case that a lot of what makes me chuckle most delightedly when I read this poem remains a private joke between us—for instance, the sly pun on 'fugitive' (Nashville being where Ransom and Tate and the other self-styled Fugitives came together 50 years ago); or the switched allusion to my own book of many years ago, *Articulate Energy*; or, best of all, our shared admiration for that neglected masterpiece, Janet Lewis's *Wife of Martin Guerre*. I suppose a really devoted or perversely diligent commentator could winkle out these allusions. What he wouldn't know, which affected me from the first very poignantly, is that you and I don't in fact know each other at all well; that we haven't been comrades-in-arms in any of the parochial squabbles and skirmishes of literary London; that in fact, when we were both young, we were lined up on sides that were taken to be, or took themselves to be, opposed. Thus the salute comes to me across a distance, from a quarter where I had no reason to expect it. And thus, despite the charming and very tactful intimacy of your addressing me, it is a public gesture—from Abse, poet, to Davie, poet. This moves me and gratifies me much more than if we had been, as it were, 'old chums.'

But Dannie, it isn't an easy poem, you know that. Though I responded at once to the affection behind the poem, and also to its technical audacity (more about that in a minute), I had to live with it for quite a long time, returning to it time and again, before I could be reasonably sure I had grasped every one of its turns and twists. I think you knew that this was the sort of poem you had written, and that you intended that I and presumably others should mull over it. For that matter, even if the poem had been addressed to some one quite different, the surprising shape and run of it

137

would, I'm convinced, have hung in my memory, teasing me, demanding that I come back to it over and over, until I possessed it as a whole. I'll try to say (it's the least I can do) what that whole is which I now think that I possess.

First, yes it is true: nothing is so 'way out' (that already dated idiom of the 1960s!) as staying in, or holding by, the centre. That centre is not necessarily nor even probably London—not for a Jew from Cardiff, nor for a Yorkshireman self-exiled to Music City, USA. But also the centre you speak of and speak from is not chiefly, let alone exclusively, a *political* centre; you are not addressing me from the middle-of-the-road, as for instance a member of the SDP/Liberal Alliance. That may be your political allegiance, as it might be mine; but that's not what you are speaking about. You are quite clear about this: the centre that you speak from, where you ask me to join you (and I will, most eagerly), is a position that is only within limits 'hygienic', a centre that is ready to settle for being, much of the time, *soiled*, dirtied by compromise, even by self-contradiction. And yes, indeed I will join you there; not in literary politics, any more than in national and international politics, can either of us afford the luxury of the purist, the absolutist, the sea-green incorruptible. By abjuring that luxury we shall lose those many readers who look to poets (since their actions have no consequences) to purvey to them the absolutism, the hygienically and murderously pure idealism, that they know it is too dangerous to tolerate in politicians. So be it; we lose those readers, but we keep our self-respect.

As regards literary or more generally artistic politics, yes, it is true that as a matter of historical fact the avant-garde can be seen to run in a circle. As the historical memory shortens in each generation, and in each generation less and less educational energy is expended on preserving that memory and transmitting it (yes, I know I sound like a crusted Tory, but bear with me), the pitiful circularity of 'the progressive' becomes more patent. You and I are old enough to have seen what was new in Paris in the 1880s applauded as unprecedented in London and New York and San Francisco of the 1960s. And yet the circle must be broken somewhere, if only because 1982 is a never wholly foreseeable breaking-out from the circle of 1981; and the myth of the avant-garde—I am ready to call it a myth—preserves that truth or that aspiration, tries to second-guess the future, and to that extent preserves, however fatuously, the cardinal virtue: HOPE.

Czeslaw Milosz, advancing an argument that I am leery of, about 'the traditional alliance between artists and revolutionaries,' says about revolutionaries: 'Their deed is equivalent to the creative act of an artist; it lifts them above themselves by demanding full surrender: *no one puts words on paper or paint on canvas doubting; if one doubts, one does so five minutes later.*' The emphasis, dear Dannie, is mine. You did not doubt, did not hesitate nor tot up possible audience-reaction, when you launched yourself on that *datum*, that 'given,' so extraordinarily unpromising both in diction and rhythm:

> *Wigged gluttony never your style but will you*
> *always eschew,*
> *barbered, the anorexia of fanaticism?*

Remember how it was when you wrote the poem. I may be thoroughly wide of the mark, but I envisage you staring at these two lines, and just trusting (to Providence, I suppose) that if you stayed with this bit of language, ungainly and all as it seemed in isolation, further configurations of language would accrue so as to make sense of it, make music of it. As happened, as duly happened. You and I know how rare in modern Britain is this capacity for not courage exactly, but hope, trust. And we know that this is not an argument for unmetred verse as against metrical verse, nor for unrhymed as against rhyming verse; for a bizarre rhyme can constitute precisely such an unlooked-for *datum*, challenging us to stay with it and make sense of it. And so, if in these reflections on the avant-garde I have gone beyond what your poem *says*, I will maintain I have not gone beyond what your poem *is*.

It was—isn't this what you mean?—the puritan in you, not the purist but the undaunted MR. HOPEFUL, who accepted this unpromising *datum*, trusting to build out of it or upon it a poem, against the odds? And as you say, one travels on the unpremeditated arc of such a poem uneasily, reluctantly, 'uneasy/sometimes as if I travelled without ticket.' Not every one feels that. The self-appointed shamans among our contemporaries apparently feel no qualms about such irruptions into, or interruptions of, the always precarious rule of rationality. As a physician, you cannot be so indulgent towards the medicineman; you have to stay, though 'way out,' still 'in the centre.' And I honour you for that, because I share the same apprehensions—for which, after all, the name might be not timidity but humility, even reverence. Hope, though in humility—it is not a bad banner to march under, though no stiff wind will unfurl it wide enough to attract the crowds round the medicine-man's totem-pole.

And after all, Dannie, what a privilege it is to be chosen (we know it isn't we who choose) to serve this ancient and unprofitable calling. I return the salute that you sent me—alas in less shapely fashion, but with all my heart just the same.

Donald Davie

Before the Last Flowers and Flies Descend

THEODORE WEISS

It should be easy for me to write about Dannie Abse, both the poet and the man. But my recollections promptly swell with details almost too busy, too multiple, too interwoven for words. His work, through which I met him first, won me with its immediacy, its colloquial idiom somewhere between the conventionalities of English verse and the licence common to the American style. Meeting in London, we instantly became good friends with the kind of recognition that would seem to presuppose a long prior history. Whenever possible we have met in England and the United States.

For a year Dannie Abse was a poet-in-residence at Princeton University. During his sojourn one of my most vivid memories occurred, one involving our travelling together on a little reading tour, chiefly in Rhode Island. Shortly after arriving we took an exploratory walk—Rhode Island was as new to me as to him—in a suburban part of Providence. It was a misty, English-countryside-like day. As we strolled along, few others in sight, the sea beating away in the distance, our talk plunged deeper and deeper, no doubt into such basic matters as the importance of place to poets and poetry. A matter especially fraught with complications for two poets long out of their native haunts. Looking up, we discovered, sheepishly enough that for all our discernment, we recognized no hint of where we had come from or how to return. Our would-be short walk required not more than an hour and several queries to retrace our way. Later, at our reading at Brown University, we so delicately respected each other's feelings we had trouble getting started.

More recently I read with Dannie Abse and four other English poets in England, at Stratford-on-Avon, during its annual Shakespeare conference. It was exciting, if not a little awing, to be reading in the Bard's home-town; but there I had brought home to me what I knew but never felt so strongly—the very considerable distance between British and American poetry. As I read the poems of M. L. Rosenthal and William Meredith, Americans who had been invited but who could not attend, and my own, it was clear that British poets and American are indeed birds together but, having nested far afield of each other, of a substantially different feather and voice. British poets, on the whole, continue to write with the outside world taken for granted; Americans tend to write from inside out—that is, if they do get out. The English still enjoy a sense of audience, of poetry's being a public occasion. Americans, less aware of, less concerned with, such focus, spend their energies on the poem itself, its inner life, its verbal resources. Small wonder American poems are often hard to grasp. So, with amusing coincidence, though Dannie Abse and I had chosen to write poems on Prospero's last days in Milan (our assignment was to write a poem on some aspect of Shakespeare or his work), his poem briskly, wryly, presented Prospero grumblingly awry in a modern old folks home, while mine concentrated on Prospero's confusion of his bewildered, lonely present with his island past.

After this event we sped to Ogmore-by-sea in Wales, to the Abse home there. A burst water main in the house hardly interrupted our pleasure in the place itself with its grand view of the sea from the living room. Our walks on the nearby cliffs, among the free-flowing sheep, their omnipresent bleatings, and the as present maze of droppings that would have driven Hansel and Gretel mad, were, despite uniformly grey, foggy days, as idyllic as one could wish. We also enjoyed being with Dannie Abse in his native habitat.

I can claim Dannie Abse, then, as a friend, yet when it comes to writing about Dannie Abse's works our very friendship makes for problems. Most obviously friendship reduces the objectivity generally thought essential for dealing with a writer. Are his writings not colored past themselves by such personal knowledge? Even so, whatever distance may seem to stretch between a man and his work, I consider our friendship a happy advantage. For it takes me at once to the heart of what I would be eager to tell anyone about Dannie Abse, poet as well as man. In a dark, mean age in which the value of humankind itself seems much in question—not why, O Lord, do you torture man as why is he obsessed with torturing others and himself and why was he visited upon the poor racked earth and himself in the first place—a poet like Dannie Abse becomes inordinately valuable indeed, precious at any time, since man is forever preoccupied with destructiveness. There is a warmth in him that informs and irradiates his work. One of the most winsome poets alive, he is little given to the explosive rigors, the violences and outrages, that possess some of his contemporaries or to the negative rigors, the rejections and denials, normal to others. He has found a middle position, one passionately aware yet patient in the face of our times' overwhelming horrors. In fact, he is one of the best present practitioners of the negative capability that I know.

Dannie Abse's training and practice as a doctor have been, I am sure, fundamentally pertinent. Even as doctoring has kept him in the presence of human suffering, it has deepened his concern for others (though he honestly, humanly admits in 'The doctor,' 'Guilty, he does not always like his patients.'), a concern that brings him into close relation with them. Where else are they encountered so nakedly, so existentially? At the same time by his training and practice he has been brought to a pitch of concentration, observation, precision and, finally, judgment that poets need but few fully attain. And not least of all to a balance, a sanity science assumes. Long ago Aristotle assured us that poets are to be respected as they make connections in the world. Abse as poet and physician is constantly on the look out for such connections, often life and death ones.

His scientific training is, however, tempered by his feelingfulness. His humanity asserts itself powerfully here. And humbly too. In his poem 'X-ray' he admits that, unlike the great men of medicine, passionate in their pursuit of knowledge, 'I am their slowcoach colleague, half afraid, / incurious.' With his mother's X-ray before him, 'My eyes look / but I don't want to; I still don't want to know.' When in 'A Winter Visit' his ninety year old mother tells him 'I would die,' then complains, 'This winter I'm half dead, son,' though crying at the accuracy of her statement is what he would do, instead, since he inhabits a white coat not a black and is a poet,

> *So I speak of small approximate things,*
> *of how I saw, in the park, four flamingoes*
> *standing, one-legged on ice, heads beneath wings.*

Earlier in the poem he had wondered whether he dared 'affirm to her' ('affirm' is most apposite here), 'so agèd and so frail, / that from one pale dot of peacock's sperm / spring forth all the colours of a peacock's tail?'

Liking his patients or not, he knows the doctor's superiority to himself in his moments of professionality:

> *so this man's politics, how he may crawl*
> *to superiors, do not matter. A doctor must care*
> *and the wife's on her knees in useless prayer,*
> *the young daughter's like a waterfall.*

Even as he quiets the man's dog, at this moment become a symbolic creature, Cerberus (though that may be the dog's normal name as well! A few lines later the situation is neatly reversed: the patient expects the doctor to be 'cheerfully sure, / to transform tremblings, gigantic unease, / by naming like a pet some small disease / with a known aetiology, certain cure.' That pet can at a moment's notice become a deadly monster), with the ominous, terrible truth, 'Soon enough you'll have a bone / or two,' the poem concludes with prescriptions potent in their poetic content and application:

> *So the doctor will and yes he will prescribe*
> *the usual dew from a banana leaf; poppies and*
> *honey too; ten snowflakes or something whiter*
> *from the bole of a tree; the clearest water*
> *ever, melting ice from a mountain lake;*
> *sunlight from waterfall's edge, rainbow smoke;*
> *tears from eyelashes of the daughter.*

For those close to the point of death, only prescriptions of life, the world itself affirmed and vividly, lovingly administered, will do.

But how, one might well wonder, aside from his nature, his gifts, and his medical experience, has Dannie Abse become the poet he is. Especially in a time as grim as ours. His ability, I would say, has been midwifed by his unusual local circumstances, on the face of it not inevitably positive: first, his birth, childhood, and youth in Wales; then, behind that, his being born a Jew. In England such a background does not automatically ensure a headstart. Furthermore, his growing up in the crackling shadow of another Welsh poet, amid the razzle-dazzle of his worldwide fame, could not have been regarded, to begin with, as an advantage. Beyond the anxiety such a presence is likely to produce, by the way he, Dylan Thomas, seemed to crowd all space and with his stentorian voice claim all attention, he must have exerted a gravity seemingly irresistible in dragging a younger poet into his stormy orbit. Certainly the young Abse was influenced by the expansive rhetoric of Dylan Thomas. But Dannie Abse soon recognized that influence's dangers. Breaking free, he succeeded in devoting himself to a stricter muse, even as he developed his native wit, the elfishly winning quality that emanates from his person and his verse, the gentle, generous unpredictability. Intelligence and craft have taken him the good way he has gone.

Beyond that, being Jewish has also helped to establish in him a sense of distance, if not difference. It has enabled him to undertake his charming expropriations of Jewish characters in his own past as in his people's history. The wedding of Welshman and Jew in him is not only unique, but uniquely attractive. The fantasy, a touch of the old whimsy too, of the Welsh, ballasted by the earthiness, the broad humor and self-awareness, of the Jew, these, playing together, even as they season his poetry, make Dannie Abse especially right for his time: a foreigner or refugee—as all now are—at home like that great ur-refugee at large, that Welshman in illimitable curiosity, tongue, mother wit, Odysseus. Or as Dannie Abse puts it himself, 'here I am in England way out in the centre.' So he asks Donald Davie, a rooted, much-traveling poet, 'Is home only home away from it?' Abse's canniness, his good earth sense, the so uncommon sense and tenacity of his origins make him, impressively enough, as much at home in his time and place as one can be. He takes for granted, so writes most successfully of, the cosmopolitan world he has lived in for years.

English poets, particularly recent ones, tend, like their American counterparts, to look askance at eloquence and high-minded sentiments. So some years ago a well-known English poet-novelist of Abse's generation, when I mentioned Dylan Thomas in my garden, could do no more than redden furiously and sputter—this long after Thomas's death—'That, that LIAR!' Our age obliges one to sympathize with modern artists' refusal to be taken in. Add to this the customary pragmatism of the English mind, its rejection of the transcendental, the Mallarméan 'something else,' or for that matter the ambition of Pound and Eliot, and we can understand why English poetry is what it is at present. Dannie Abse shares some measure of his contemporaries' hard-headedness. In his latest volume's first poem, 'Smile please,' he admits that when he was young he trafficked in the mythical:

> *I'd catch Leda naked, her face flushed,*
> *her body white like the swan's; or wrathful*
> *Apollo erect and frustrated as Daphne*
> *became less woman, more tree.*

Once he was available to and excited by such allusions. But now, convinced of the superior authority, the inimitable appeal, of experience itself, he declares:

> *Older, it's scenes like this that charm me—the disguise*
> *of comedy, blossom of a nettle, a wedding photograph!*
> *And tonight I'll show you the touched-up proof*
> *as new-minted Mr and Mrs kiss and kiss*
>
> *to prove no developed metamorphosis*
> *can be as wild or as genuine as this.*

Tongue in cheeky business this may be, but his punning tongue knows its basic business, never wholly abandons it. Similarly in 'Orpheus in the surgery,' stripping the ur-poet, putting him to the knife, Orpheus is made to confess that he lied. For turning, he found himself alone: 'It was I, not she, who whispered, "Who?" ' Dannie Abse acknowledges the limitations of poetry. His work does include the celebratory but with his eyes wide open. We know his generation's great predecessor Auden's respect for common sense, his aversion to 'empty sonorities,' his reprobation of his youthful whoring after lies. The truthfulness of things as they are principally concern such poets. With life as fragile and threatened as it is today, how do more than admit this fact, let alone—as the now distant modernists of the Rilke variety insisted—attempt to change that life? Whatever his Welshhood, Dannie Abse is hardly seduced by

146

free-floating fantasy. So his witty, deflating 'Pantomime diseases' with its trenchant puns:

> *When the three Darling children thought they'd fly*
> *to Never-Never-Land—the usual trip—*
> *their pinpoint pupils betrayed addiction.*
> *And not hooked by Captain Hook but by*
> *that ponce, Peter Pan! All the rest is fiction.*

Some of Dannie Abse's contemporaries seem to me in danger of being victims of their time, convinced by what they often hate and regret, and correspondent with those theoreticians, continental and otherwise, who consider poetry a word game, not in touch—as its parent language cannot be—with any reality beyond itself. In this shrinkage the poet, like a drowning man, is likely to clutch the personal or domestic scene, the little world immediately available to him. Modesty, though appealing in itself, is questionable as a desideratum for poetry. Yet almost inevitably it becomes the prevailing mien. Such poetry, by what it shrugs off, is bound to substantiate the theoreticians' disparaging view of it. Fortunately Dannie Abse's love of language, the richness of his heritage, and the feelingfulness welling out of these, guarantee a sense of the copiousness of the world in his work. Though his book's last poem, 'Last words,' twitting literature's heroes and heroines on their death-bed theatrics, has it,

> *And how would I wish to go?*
> *Not as in opera—that would offend—*
> *nor like a blue-eyed cowboy shot and short of words,*
> *but finger-tapping still our private morse, '. . . love you,'*
> *before the last flowers and flies descend.*

Dannie Abse knows, with a poet altogether wary of exaggeration and pretense, Marianne Moore, 'What is more precious than precision? Illusion.' So even Auden has said,

> *. . .only*
> *Those who love illusion*
> *And know it will go far:*
> *Otherwise we spend our*

> *Lives in a confusion*
> *Of what we say and do with*
> *Who we really are.*

Abse's work delights in the play of the mind, language in its resourcefulness, those mintings as sweet in the mouth and the mind as anything else—words. He knows what we add to life through our feelings and our thoughts (like the bird's song and the tree's leaves), and also through the arts and that paramount human faculty, now most embattled, by which the arts prosper, the imagination. But imagination never divorced from the earth.

And if, with the lights of our civilization virtually out, we are blind together in this present darkness at noon, Dannie Abse believes like his learned Rabbi Yose (yet misunderstanding by his very endless pondering of the Torah's 'Thou shalt grope at noonday / as the blind gropeth in darkness,' for he fails to realize that it means the blind, not in the night, but in the dark of their blindness) that we still can brandish torches as we move inside our darkness so that others see us, and we save each other

> *from quicksand and rock, from the snake asleep,*
> *from cactus, from thistle and from thornbush,*
> *from the deep potholes in the roadway.*

Dannie Abse and his work flourish such a torch. Not only rocks and quicksand and potholes have been lit up, but the lovely landscapes of friendship and affection, otherwise invisible. Or without these torches a world terribly diminished, if not entirely lost.

Conversations with Dannie Abse

1

The first interview took place at the end of May, 1982, over the long bank holiday. The weather was warm with sustained sunshine, and Dr. Dannie Abse and I talked at length sitting in his garden behind his home in Golders Green. The irises had reached their peak and were fading, but the roses were in their first full bloom when we held our discussions, not unaware that this particular weekend was marked by other dimensions than literary ones. For the Pope's visit to England had just begun, and in the Falkland Islands, the British assault to retake Port Stanley was underway. The seriousness of these historical matters notwithstanding, we began our leisurely discussion.

J. C. You've shown me the letter that Hutchinson's wrote to you, September 5th, 1946, saying that they accepted *After Every Green Thing*, your first book of poems, for publication. You were a medical student at the time. You must have been delighted.

D. A. Yes, but Hutchinson's took over two years before they actually published *After Every Green Thing*—the title, by the way, comes from the Book of Job . . . the ass that goes after every green thing.

J. C. Those early poems were very romantic, indeed lush. They show a vitality of imagery, much that's memorable, yet mostly they're immature. I assume you agree for you've only included one of them, 'The Uninvited' in your *Collected Poems*.

D. A. Yes, they *are* immature. I was immature. I caught like an infection, the neo-romantic fashionable mode of the time.

J.C. How would you characterise the qualities of these neo-romantic poets? Were they much influenced by Dylan Thomas?

D.A. Grigson who was antagonistic to Dylan Thomas's poetry thundered that 'the romance we are drifting back to is a romance without reason, it is altogether self-indulgent and liquescent.' Those poets contributing to neo-romantic periodicals such as *Poetry Quarterly* held Dylan Thomas in high regard and were much less gifted than he. Their diction was florid, rhetorical, and their subject matter often wilfully obscure—due to an excessively private vision. This was the case sometimes, too, with Dylan Thomas.

J.C. Yet some of these young *Poetry Quarterly* poets like Alex Comfort and Denise Levertov had real talent. I believe you were a friend of Alex Comfort's?

D.A. Alex Comfort had shown me—he was a little older than me—nothing but kindness. And Denise Levertov who was my exact contemporary was a friend.

J.C. Did you and Levertov discuss poetry together?

D.A. As a matter of fact there is one poem in *After Every Green Thing* that was—perhaps I can admit to it now—addressed to Denise Levertov. It begins 'Lady of black hair I see you dead in a red dress.' That lady of black hair was Denise Levertov.

J.C. That poem isn't in your *Collected Poems*. So would you read it out loud.

D.A. It's not very . . .

J.C. Never mind.

D.A.

> *'Lady of black hair I see you dead in a red dress,*
> *I bend over to kiss your face of ivory in moonlight,*
> *I touch your ache of branches weighted with fruit.*
>
> *I touch your fruit. What terrible cry is this?*
> *You open the gangrene of birds in your breasts,*
> *in pain of roses you open your mouth to speak.*
>
> *And think, all these years you have been dead,*
> *wonderfully silent in a red dress,*
> *beautifully white and dead in moonlight.*

I am in no way accustomed to a corpse speaking.

I cannot enter and walk through the mists,
and depart as both boy and girl, alive as a voice,
with my eyes in terror of two worlds.

I cannot follow the music out of the room,
leaving those I love, standing there, gesticulating,
and return, return as before, sane and accepted.

For I should not speak again being of two sexes,
being knowledgeable with the terror of two worlds.
I know no man who has lived in a female grave.

And think, all these years you have been dead,
wonderfully silent in a red dress,
beautifully white and dead in moonlight.

I am in no way accustomed to a corpse speaking.'

J. C. That's a very odd, a very erotic poem.

D. A. Not long before I wrote it I learnt from my elder brother, Leo, who's $6\frac{1}{2}$ years older than me, that between his birth and mine my mother had had a miscarriage, a stillbirth, a girl. I was 22 or 23 when I learnt this surprising news and had recently met Denise Levertov with whom I felt much in common. For instance, Denise's mother was a very Welsh, Welsh lady and her father a Russian Jew who'd become a Church of England Divine. So this background of hers, Welsh and Jewish, made me feel kinship with her. Besides we were both writing poetry in that neo-romantic tradition; also our political views were not too dissimilar. And she had been a nurse and I was a medical student.

J. C. I didn't know she'd been a nurse.

D. A. She tended to think in the same way as I did—saw the same face in a cloud, the same pattern in a carpet. I suddenly began to have the extraordinary feeling that Denise Levertov was an embodiment of the dead-at-birth sister that I never knew.

J. C. 'I am in no way accustomed to a corpse speaking.'

D. A. When I published the poem in *Poetry Quarterly* I received a few letters from homosexual readers who, misunderstanding the poem, thought I was declaring that I was homosexual or bisexual. It so

153

happens I've not had a homosexual experience in my life—nevertheless, I recognize, as Freud tells us, that we all have within us a masculine and a feminine component and in that poem I was unconsciously projecting this; though consciously, in a private way, I was only referring to my dead sister and Denise Levertov—I might add that my feelings spoilt my relationship with Denise. I was a promiscuous young man, but I had a feeling that Denise, attractive as she was, was not for me, that to make overtures to her would . . .

J. C. Would have been incestuous?

D. A. That's right.

J. C. That's very interesting because if you had not mentioned this personal aspect, there'd be no way of knowing . . .

D. A. Yes, it's too private. One should eschew such private references in poetry.

J. C. But there are several things that are not merely private which came through to me as you read the poem, among them the combined feminine and masculine principles. As I said, it's a very erotic poem.

D. A. Necrophilic?

J. C. The poem succeeds in that it recognizes the masculine and feminine aspects of ourselves. It recognizes that duality, I'm reminded of Tiresias, and the use of him made by Eliot and Durrell. By the way, you never had in the back of your head the image of the Sleeping Beauty when you wrote that poem?

D. A. No, not at all. Of course, for all I know Sleeping Beauty had a mother who before she was born had a miscarriage!

J. C. O.K. Whereas I think 'Lady of black hair' succeeds, I know many of the others fail. For instance, I've read a lot of war poems, but your early war poem, 'Tonight slippers of darkness fall,' is about the worst one I've ever read.

D. A. O.K.

J. C. The best quality in this first book is its lyrical intensity—and a more controlled lyricism is evident in your later work. Your poem 'Epithalamion,' comes to mind, though that, also, is quite an early poem. It was published in your second book *Walking Under Water*

154

which contains poems written between 1948 and 1951. You were still a medical student.

D. A. I qualified in 1950.

J. C. *Walking Under Water* shows little *stylistic* development. There are more successes in it than the previous volume but many poems are flawed and most are still neo-romantic in tone. There are exceptions. A poem like 'Letter to Alex Comfort' about the nature of scientific inspiration and its misapplication of scientific knowledge to war technology is cast in a less intense way, is more relaxed in diction.

D. A. Yes, that poem is more conversationally pitched. It's a drier, wittier poem than the more hortatory poems I was then, in 1948, tending to write. 'Letter to Alex Comfort' in some ways predates the Movement poetry of the fifties—all those Movement poems you can find in the 1956 *New Lines* anthology edited by Robert Conquest which included the then 'new' poets, Larkin, Donald Davie, etc. Their poems, also, tried for a more chaste diction, a more neutral tone.

J. C. Conquest, I seem to remember, claimed their poems had a more intellectual backbone than the neo-romantic poetry of the Forties, and owned a 'notable aridity.'

D. A. 'Letter to Alex Comfort' has in it such lines as 'Ehrlich certainly was one who broke down the mental doors' and 'Koch also, painfully and with true German thoroughness / eliminated the impossible.' I mean there was a naming of names. Seven years later, the Movement poets were writing lines like 'That was not what Berkeley meant.'

J. C. By?

D. A. By Donald Davie. Thom Gunn began one of his poems, 'Shelley was drowned near here.' D. J. Enright began one, 'Was Freud entirely right?' Then worst of all there's Conquest's

> *Perhaps Karlsefni saw it to starboard*
> *On the voyage to Hop from Straumfjord.*

J. C. Ha ha ha.

D. A. Such naming of names became for a while a Movement tic.

155

But I hope that in 'Letter to Alex Comfort,' the naming of names was not simply name-dropping. Nor, though conversationally pitched, was the diction of that poem too arid.

J. C. In succeeding years your diction has varied from the more relaxed language of 'Letter to Alex Comfort' to the lyrical intensity of 'Epithalamion.' I've always found that poem to be especially appealing which accounts, I suppose, for its being frequently anthologised. I assume it came out of actual experience. Do you recall that marvellous passage right at the end of Molly Bloom's soliloquy in *Ulysses* where she's reminiscing about her courtship with Bloom and says 'they might as well try to stop the sun from rising tomorrow the sun shine for you he said the day we were lying among the rhododendrons on Howth head in the grey tweed suit and his straw hat the day I got him to propose to me yes first I gave him the bit of seedcake out of my mouth and it was leapyear like now yes 16 years ago my God after that long kiss I near lost my breath yes he said I was a flower of the mountain yes so we are flowers all a womans body yes. . . But to get back to your barleyfield.

D. A. I don't recall ever making love to a girl in a *barley* field! You know some months after I wrote that poem I happened on a paper in a psychoanalytical journal called 'Barley, Wedding Rings and Styes in the Eye.'

J. C. Styes in the Eye?

D. A. I mentioned earlier about my mother being pregnant, a still-birth. Another thing I learnt about my mother's pregnancies—was that, one each occasion, my father developed a stye in the eye. It was a family joke. So when I came across that psychoanalytical paper I read it with interest. It pointed out that a primitive method of treating styes in the eye was by rubbing them with a golden wedding ring—and that to this day golden eye-ointment is used to treat styes though that ointment is a weak antiseptic and there are many better ones.

J. C. Barley too is golden.

D. A. It's a fertility symbol. So 'my white girl in a barley field' is apt—though in placing her in that topography I did so without awareness of such a thing.

J. C. It was unconscious.

156

D. A. Yes. Incidentally, after I read that paper, while a medical student, I must have been a nuisance in the Ophthalmology Department. For whenever I encountered a man with a stye in his eye, I asked him if his wife or mistress had missed a period!

J. C. May I turn now to the poems 1951–1956 which you collected in *Tenants of the House*, a volume which shows a significant advance on the two previous volumes? *Tenants of the House* has shaken off the neo-romantic mannerisms, it's a highly individual volume, as Edwin Muir indicated when he reviewed it; and I'm not surprised it's the first book of yours, poems I mean, to be published in the U.S.A.

D. A. Many of the poems in *Tenants* used an allegorical or a symbolic framework. I got into the habit of working that way, off and on, for about a decade so such poems are to be found also in my next book *Poems, Golders Green* published in 1962.

J. C. Yes, I think *Poems, Golders Green* is a transitional book linking your later work to your earlier. But what do you mean by allegorical?

D. A. On one level I was saying one particular thing, on another something more general.

J. C. You were writing about mountaineering in 'The Mountaineers' but really referring to the creative process rather as Frost did in his poem 'Apple-Picking'.

D. A. I wrote about mountaineers, yes, but as you rightly say I was thinking about the creative process. I wrote about a particular football game in Cardiff but was referring to the evil and good propensities in man, how they were in conflict with each other. I sang a song about five men warring over a deserted island—territory something like the Falkland Islands—but I was really making a noise about the danger of a nuclear holocaust. Such poems were simple parables, allegories. Other poems in that same volume were symbolically ordered.

J. C. By which you mean? The difference between allegorically ordered and symbolically ordered?

D. A. The difference is between a sign and a symbol. 'X' can be a sign or a symbol. It can be an emblem and stand for one particular

157

thing or 'X' can stand for many things and remain finally an enigma. Poems like 'The Trial,' for instance, cannot be totally paraphrased, as can say 'The Mountaineers,' or 'Emperors of the Island.'

J.C. Still 'The Trial' comes through in a concrete way. It's an existentialist ballad.

D.A. Yes, in the 50s' I was interested in existentialist literature, in Sartre, in Camus, and how they dramatised philosophical questions.

J.C. Do you maintain that interest in existentialism? You continue to touch on the theme of absurdity—the absurdity of existence in the 20th century.

D.A. Indeed. In 'Lunch and Afterwards' the protagonist in that recent poem, on learning from a pathologist how after death, the first organ to disappear is the brain and how the last organ to endure is the uterus, finds that he needs to *act*. So he, standing next to a telephone, thinks of a number, then doubles it. It's an act, even though it is one of total absurdity.

J.C. I think there's a lot of despair in that recent poem and I recall how, when I first read *Tenants of the House* years ago I was aware of how much despair about the human condition haunted the poems—and that despair seems to be a part of the whole existentialist *gestalt*.

D.A. I wouldn't admit to unrelenting despair in *Tenants of the House*. You'll find lines in such poems as 'Poem of Celebration' as:

> *Any man may gather the images of despair.*
> *I'll say 'I will' and 'I can'*
> *and, like an accident, breathe in space and air.*

In the next volume, *Poems, Golders Green*, there are lines from 'The Grand View' which read

> *There are moments when a man must praise*
> *the astonishment of being alive,*
> *when small mirrors of reality blaze*
> *into miracles. . .*

158

I've known the mood of jubilation and the mood of despair. Who hasn't? My poems reflect that. True, as the years turn over the pages, my poems become more sombre. My consciousness of recent history: the nuclear crimes in Nagasaki, Hiroshima; the crimes of Auschwitz, Dachau; the geography of Vietnapalm; the awful opening mouths of the lethal crowd; this awareness does not diminish with the years. On the contrary.

J.C. You are talking about general and public aggressiveness. But 'The Trial' postulates an individual helplessness, an existential despair. He who is on trial for throwing off his masks will be found guilty, will be hung. He may be hung high, he may be hung low, but he'll be hung.

D.A. That's so.

J.C. I think 'The Second Coming' suggests a similar despair. I find this poem enormously interesting in several respects. You seem to suggest that people expecting a messiah are deluding themselves. The saviour emerges from the earth like an old vegetation god to get his head lopped off by the technology of our civilisation. This killing machinery precludes the possibility of a spiritual rebirth.

D.A. Yes.

J.C. Are you aware also of the affinities it has with a couple of Dylan Thomas's poems? The one about the birth of the baby who, emerging, utters 'If my head hurt a hair's foot.' Also that other Thomas poem which begins 'Light breaks where no sun shines.' In 'The Second Coming' you have the line, 'Still his body in darkness, lightward pushing.'

D.A. I'm happy to acknowledge influences where I see them, and Dylan Thomas was an early influence, but the line of mine you quote owes much more to my experience, experience of delivering babies, rather than reading Dylan Thomas.

J.C. It is finally, in some ways, a political poem. I'm struck, as a matter of fact, by how many of the poems in *Tenants of the House* are political. There's a consciousness of the obligation to resist the official destructive forces of the twentieth century. Daniel in the lion's den must reject these value systems, must remain a maverick and resist being murdered.

159

D.A. I would have liked to have written more political or rather more public poems. There are a few in *Tenants of the House* and those there are do proclaim my continuing emotional imperative of 'oppose, oppose orthodoxies.' 'Outside is a lonely place.'

J.C. Yes, from 'New Babylons':

> Let spellbound lions know
> an angel in the den
> lest they bite to please
> the vast majorities.
>
> Outside is a lonely place.

D.A. When I wrote those lines I more frequently leaned on mythological references. Since *A Small Desperation* I think I've written much more directly.

J.C. I recall that in writing about *A Small Desperation* Jeremy Robson observed that you explore those areas of experience which defy articulation. That observation's true, I think, not only for *A Small Desperation* but for many poems written since then. For instance, in that dialogue poem 'Hunt the Thimble' you allude to mysteries we all perceive but cannot explain. It seems in such poems you're trying to probe the reality beyond our general, commonplace reality. You seem to be moving toward defining the undefinable. May we discuss 'Hunt the Thimble'? First I'll read the whole poem out loud:

> Hush now. You cannot describe it.
>
> Is it like heavy rain falling,
> and lights going on, across the fields,
> in the new housing estate?
>
> Cold, cold. Too domestic, too
> temperate, too devoid of history.
>
> Is it like a dark windowed street at night,
> the houses uncurtained, the street deserted?
>
> Colder. You are getting colder,
> and too romantic, too dream-like.
> You cannot describe it.

The brooding darkness then,
that breeds inside a cathedral
of a provincial town in Spain?

In Spain, also, but not Spanish.
In England, if you like, but not English.
It remains, even when obscure, perpetually.
Aged, but ageless, you cannot describe it.
No, you are cold, altogether too cold.

Aha—the blue sky over Ampourias,
the blue sky over Lancashire for that matter . . .

You cannot describe it.

. . . obscured by clouds?
I must know what you mean.

Hush, hush.

Like those old men in hospital dying,
who, unaware strangers stand around their bed,
stare obscurely, for a long moment,
at one of their own hands raised—
which perhaps is bigger than the moon again—
and then, drowsy, wandering, shout out, 'Mama'.

Is it like that? Or hours after that even:
the darkness inside a dead man's mouth?

No, no, I have told you:
you are cold, and you cannot describe it.

D. A. For many years I've been interested in reinhabiting sensual experience, the furthest evidence of our senses. I've been interested, as it were, in olfactory pursuits and in the delineation of mood. When *A Small Desperation* was published the reviewer in *The Times* was kind enough to say that 'Hunt the Thimble' was a small masterpiece, and he described it as a dialogue that took place inside a mortuary. I'm not eager to contradict him about the poem being a small masterpiece but that the dialogue took place in a mortuary was news to me! As far as I'm concerned, it's a dialogue where one person asks another—a human being or an oracle, a sphinx, or a

161

god—unanswerable questions. We all have a need, at times, to ask unanswerable questions.

J. C. The image of 'the darkness inside a dead man's mouth' is very striking. And so is that of the old men in hospital dying, shouting out 'Mama' and staring at their own hand raised 'which is bigger than the moon again.'

D. A. Most of those images are drawn from experience. Dying men do sometimes call for their mothers, do raise their hands and stare at them, surprised almost, as babies in prams do. When we're very young we think the moon is smaller than our hand because when we raise it up it can blot out the moon from our vision.

J. C. It's getting back to primitive thinking, something you do frequently—as in 'Mysteries.'

D. A. But the thought, primitive or not, is rooted in actuality. I ended 'Mysteries' with the line, 'I start with the visible and am startled by the visible.'

J. C. Are you aware how, in 'Mysteries,' after its initial statement of 'At night, I do not know who I am / when I dream, when I am sleeping' you bounce back from an audible experience to a visual one consistently? After you write of the audible one:

> *Awakened, I hold my breath and listen:*
> *a thumbnail scratches the other side of the wall*

you continue visually:

> *At midday, I enter a sunlit room*
> *to observe the lamplight on for no reason.*

Then comes the audible, followed by the visible notation:

> *I should know by now that few octaves can be heard,*
> *that a vision dies from being too long stared at;*

Now back to the audible:

162

> *that the whole of recorded history even*
> *is but a little gossip in a great silence;*

And so you continue in that consistent pattern, ending with the primacy of the visible.

D.A. I wasn't aware of all that.

J.C. I wonder why you didn't remain consistent and conclude with 'I start with the *audible* and am startled by the visible.'

D.A. Ha ha ha.

J.C. One of the things that interests me is the way you begin with the empirical and then go to the primitive to go beyond the empirical. You do that, for example, in the poem, 'An Old Commitment.' Here you identify yourself with kinsmen slain in battle, long long ago, and wonder why you feel such loyalties.

D.A. Loyalty can be a means of linking the present to the past.

J.C. You mean in the sense of traversing time? A summoning?

D.A. Yes. It may interest you to know—it so happens I wrote that poem in Wales after a visit to Israel. I'd been on a poetry-reading tour with several British poets including Ted Hughes. One afternoon I was walking with Ted Hughes and the Israeli poet, Yehuda Amichai, in Jerusalem not far from the mosque, the Dome of the Rock. Suddenly, without warning, Ted deliberately flung himself on to the ground. He lay horizontal, all six foot of him, his arms outstretched, face down, as he stared through a grill into blackness. And he crooned softly, 'Blackness, blackness.' He was just assing around, but it seemed to me almost—for he was so intense—as if he was trying to summon blackness up through that hole. At last he rose and noticed, on his hands, the marks the iron grill had made. He held them up to us delighted—for on his hands were the sign of the stigmata.

J.C. You conclude 'An Old Commitment' with the lines:

> *Black,' I call softly to one dead but beloved,*
> *'black, black,' wanting the night to reply . . .*

But that was a whispering, as it were, to your ancient kinsmen.

163

D. A. After we left Jerusalem we went to the Dead Sea and, on the way back, in the car, we saw bobbing above the line of mountain-tops a round orange sun. And I was reminded of another car journey I had made in Wales—the sun setting and the mountains, and ancient monuments I had passed or visited there as I had done and did in Israel.

J. C. Do you feel a kinship with Ted Hughes?

D. A. How do you mean?

J. C. Do you admire his work?

D. A. Yes. He's tremendously talented.

J. C. What about Larkin? You and Larkin have written some poems on the same subjects: returning to home-towns, mourners passing by on grey afternoons, reflections on middle-age, faith-healers.

D. A. Philip Larkin's return-journey poem to Coventry has a satiri-cal strategy. It's very cautious. He's sending up those of us who are more earnest about our return journeys. Through the use of nega-tives, he defensively tells us his boyhood daydreams and ambitions. His list of details, as ever, is wonderfully accurate. I think my own 'Return to Cardiff' has fewer affinities with the Larkin poem, 'I remember, I remember,' than with Dylan Thomas's script 'Return to Swansea' which as a piece of radio I admired immensely.

J. C. Your poem about the spiritualist is not so laid back as Larkin's. It's more angry.

D. A. I had been to interview Harry Edwards for a Sunday news-paper.

J. C. Harry . . ?

D. A. He was the leading British spiritualist. He maintained that his spirit guides were Lister and Louis Pasteur.

J. C. Oh boy!

D. A. He had a mansion in Shere, Surrey. People with progressive and terminal diseases were consulting him. They even brought their sick pets, alsatians, cats, for him to cure.

J. C. He made a lot of money ministering both to man and beast?

164

D. A. I'm sure he did.

J. C. Perhaps you responded as a physician . . . before you wrote that poem.

D. A. Yes, it's a bit like a letter . . . *Disgusted*, Harley Street. I don't think my poem and Larkin's have too much in common; but I should like to emphasise that Larkin's poems have given me much perdurable pleasure—they are so sharp-eyed and appropriate with arresting detail. Nor do they eschew sentiment, feeling.

J. C. Acknowledging Larkin's mastery of his craft, would you comment on the proposition that in his insistence on plain words and plain acts he insures part of his popularity by a vulgar appeal to the gallery in us as in lines like 'groping back to bed after a piss,' 'he's fucking her and she's / Taking pills or wearing a diaphragm' or 'They fuck you up, your mum and dad' which last line, incidentally, was just quoted in *The Sunday Times Colour Supplement* as being among his best known lines?

D. A. Er, the word 'fuck' will endure in the English language!

J. C. I sure hope so!

D. A. Not long ago, after a poetry-reading a very small lady approached me. 'You didn't swear like the poet we had here last,' she said. I wasn't sure whether she was complaining or commending me for my chaste diction. 'You don't use swear words,' she insisted, 'in your poems.' I came to the conclusion she was more disappointed than pleased. I became curious to know which poet had evidently impressed her on the previous reading at that literary society. 'Nuttall,' she told me. 'A man called Nuttall.'

J. C. Nuttall?

D. A. 'What swear words did Mr. Nuttall use?' I asked as innocently as possible. She hesitated. 'Ah,' she said finally, 'that would be telling.' Then she turned away presumably to some barracks for better verbal refreshment.

J. C. Swear words very rarely come into your poetry as a matter of fact, or for that matter in other Anglo-Welsh poets.

D. A. We are a respectable people. I remember how, in 1956, Vernon Watkins invited my wife and me to his house on the Pen-

165

nard cliffs, the Gower side of Swansea. He's been editing the correspondence between Dylan Thomas and himself for Faber and Faber. Vernon was mightily angry because an editor had censored Dylan Thomas's letters. 'He deleted,' Vernon said excitedly, 'a certain word whenever it arose and it arose frequently, for Dylan, do you see, freely used this word both in speech and in his letters.' I became aware of how aware Vernon was of my wife's presence. He resolutely stared away from her as he continued, 'It's a word that is somewhat stronger than bloody. Indeed Dylan used this word quite innocently. These days many people speak it, not merely those who are ill-bred. Readers are accustomed nowadays to read this word. Why it's hard to read a modern novel without encountering it. How dare they alter the character of Dylan's letters by censoring this word?' Vernon became more and more angry. For another two minutes he raged against his publisher—and righteous his protestations. Yet not once did Vernon being a correct and courteous man . . .

J.C. And Welsh

D.A. . . . utter, in front of my wife, that word which is so much worse than bloody.

J.C. Nor have you, for that matter. We seem to have gone off on a tangent. I'd like to return to your poetry—the fact that you're a doctor, the fact that you're a Jew, how these facts have affected your poems. All this we haven't discussed. Nor have we touched on your plays. Maybe we can continue this interview, at a later date, after you've come back from Wales and I've come back from Ireland?

D.A. Sure. Let's call it a day, now.

2

It was in middle late June, 1982, that Dannie Abse and I resumed our talk. Soon after we concluded our first conversation he went to Ogmore-by-Sea on the Bristol Channel and I went to Dublin to participate in the James Joyce Centenary Celebration. When we met again, it was with the shared feeling that with fragile truces holding the lives of people in balance in the Falklands and in Lebanon the world seemed daily to be moving farther away from the enterprise of literature.

J. C. Many have been killed in the Falklands and the Middle East since we last talked. In some parts of the world writers would be asked to proclaim on such matters.

D. A. As a matter of fact I've just been asked to contribute to a book called *Authors Take Sides on the Falklands*.

J. C. What was your view? What is your view?

D. A. When we go to war we need, of course, for sanity's sake a cause. The Greeks besieged Troy because beautiful Helen, they most sincerely believed, had been abducted, forced into a coloured ship that sailed for Troy. Yet there's another legend, another report, less sensational. Helen never went to Troy. She quit home, yes, but freely; and she travelled to Cyprus perhaps, to Egypt perhaps—and meanwhile for ten long years those Greeks and those Trojans slaughtered each other because of a fairy story, a lying headline, a ghost, an empty garment. In that piece I wrote for *Authors Take Sides on the*

167

Falklands I said that I believed this other story, that Helen was observed by tourists on the banks of a Delta. Do you know those lines of Seferis?

> *Deep girdled, the sun in her hair, with that way of*
> *   standing . . .*
> *The lively skin, the eyes and the great eyelids,*
> *She was there, on the banks of a Delta*
> *   And at Troy?*
> *Nothing. At Troy, a phantom.*
> *So the gods willed it.*
> *And Paris lay with a shadow as though it were*
> *   solid flesh:*
> *And we were slaughtered for Helen ten long years.*

J.C. Are you suggesting the Falklands war is an unnecessary one? I'm sure you don't feel sympathetic to the Argentinian government.

D.A. Of course not. They're thugs in uniform. Who can deny that? It's true, and because it's true, what a cause! What a Helen! So pass the gun, the drum and the blood drip. Te ra ra. Te ra ra!

J.C. In Auden's 'The Musée des Beaux Arts' . . .

D.A. Yes.

J.C. '. . . the expensive delicate ship that must have seen / Something amazing, a boy falling out of the sky, / Had somewhere to get to and sailed calmly on.' I mean there are terrible happenings in the world—not just in the Falklands or in Lebanon, but for most of us not directly affected we have to continue our usual routines.

D.A. We all have somewhere to go, maybe it's only to an office or to the pub, but we are obliged to say something about the disaster of Icarus if we've witnessed it.

J.C. You're saying poets have certain obligations.

D.A. First to make the best poem they can with what gift they have. But a poem has to say something. It may not have the same logic as prose but it still must refer to the real world we live in. Camus once wrote, 'The writer's role is not free of difficult duties. By definition he cannot put himself today in the service of those who make history: he is at the service of those who suffer it.' That

168

statement may sound romantic but there are occasions when it's true.

J.C. There's a poem of yours called, 'Give me your hands.' In it, you speak of personal obligations. In your case, the duties of a doctor.

D.A. I wrote that poem during the Vietnam War.

J.C. I'll read the poem:

> Scared trees, hissing in the garden,
> can't hear human voices harden.
> I can: my two neighbors quarrel.
>
> 'Mine!' 'Mine!' Nothing to do with me.
> Once more I flex my head to see
> the latest Sunday photograph.
>
> In Vietnam, beneath scarred trees,
> unreal the staring casualties.
> Of course I care. What good is that?
>
> Faint in the hall the telephone goes.
> As I approach, how loud it grows.
> I lift up a voice saying, 'Doctor?'
>
> So in a room I do not know
> I hold a hand I do not know
> for hours. Again a dry old hand.
>
> There's something else that I must do,
> for some other thing is crying too
> in chaos, near, without a name.

A war's going on in Vietnam but you indicate that though you care about 'the staring casualties' of that war, merely caring isn't good enough: you are not in Vietnam, you are elsewhere in your own life and being a doctor must be involved in compassionate conduct on a personal level.

D.A. Icarus has crashed to the ground—then it was in Vietnam, now it's in the Falklands, in Lebanon—but meanwhile the fellow *next door* is unwell and needs attention.

J.C. Is that a doctor's or poet's response?

169

D. A. It's a doctor's response if he goes next door; it's a poet's response if he makes a poem out of it. And if he's a poet and a doctor, he must do both . . .

J. C. Of all the poems in which you call on your experience as a doctor I think that sequence you called 'The Smile Was' is the most successful.

D. A. When a medical student, I attended a hundred births and noted how the new mother smiled, on hearing her child cry for the first time. I was very much struck by the purity of that smile—more pure than the archaic smile of Greek statues. So often people are ambivalent about things, but not the new mother—even if the baby had been unwanted, illegitimate, it seemed that, at least for a minute in her life, the neophyte mother knew unambiguous happiness. Her smile always signalled that.

J. C. In *A Poet in the Family* you describe how a drunken Itzig Manager praised you in one breath then, in the next, punched you on the jaw. Is that what you mean by ambiguous?

D. A. Well, ambivalence—in that case, in the relationship between flattery and aggression. I remember once travelling late at night on a train from Bristol to Cardiff. The man next to me, who'd been reading his *Daily Telegraph*, suddenly threw it aside complaining because two youngsters further down the carriage were threatening to each other. 'I can't bear violence,' he whispered to me. 'I just can't bear any kind of violence at all. I can't bear it, I can't bear it.' The youths continued to quarrel but like a good doctor, I told my whispering fellow-passenger, 'Not to worry.' Soon the train stopped and the two warring youngsters left. But on the platform they began thumping each other. Whereupon my mild fellow-passenger rose to his feet, eyes blazing and screamed, 'Kill him, murder him, kill him.'

J. C. In 'The Smile Was' you talk about an Indian patient, his mixed feelings about being given a clean bill of health. And you also refer in another section of the poem to a surgeon colleague who smiles beneath his surgical mask when he makes his first incision. You make it plain that the surgeon is a good man, a healer, yet his ambivalence is not too dissimilar from that of the man you just described in the train journey from Bristol.

170

D. A. Right.

J. C. Your preoccupation with irrational behaviour is forcefully dramatised in your long poem, *Funland*. In that poem you give us a view of a lunatic asylum from within. It really is a microcosm for the world without. Are you making a judgment here as a doctor or as a poet?

D. A. I'm not two people.

J. C. I should like to discuss *Funland* with you but I know in a previous interview you declined to explicate *Funland*.

D. A. Well I do have some sympathy with the view John Carey ventilated in a piece he called 'The Critic as Vandal.' He suggested that critics, in order to discuss a poem, reword it and in so doing vandalise it. I don't want to do that with *Funland*.

J. C. I know that essay of Carey's. He acts as an anti-critic.

D. A. Yes.

J. C. His essay is destructive. I think his argument which invalidates academic criticism in particular, and literary criticism in general, is absurd. His argument is that the critic only tampers by substituting bogus meanings in his paraphrasing. But how can I bring students to be perceptive about literature without exploring nuances of meaning?

D. A. In our first interview you pointed out how Frost referred to the creative process in 'Apple-Picking.' To be frank, I knew Frost's poem but had not read it in that way. I do think that sometimes academic critics do go to a text as if it were a code. I'm not sure that the decoding of 'Apple-Picking' helps me to enjoy that poem more. The reading of it you suggest may take away as much as it adds. True, eventually, I may be able to recapture the poem, possess it as I did in my innocence.

J. C. I don't think interpreting Frost's poem in that way diminishes the integrity of the poem.

D. A. There's an old Zen saying that 'to a man who knows nothing, mountains are mountains, waters are waters and trees are trees. But when he has studied and knows a little, mountains are no longer mountains, waters no longer waters, and trees no longer trees. But

171

when he has thoroughly understood, mountains are once again mountains, waters are waters, and trees are trees.' Too many academic critics take us only to the second stage where mountains are no longer mountains . . .'

J.C. My experience with students, of many years in the classroom is that by making certain decodings, as you put it, a deeper appreciation of the poem studied results. However, to get back to *Funland*. Would you say it was a departure from the main body and progress of your work? I don't mean just because it's a long poem.

D.A. In some ways. On the other hand it's a persona poem, and over the years I've written a number of such poems, imagining myself to be someone quite other than I am: a dispossessed upper-class owner of a stately home (in 'Social Revolution in England'); or an Israeli poet in the year 1948 or 1949 (in 'Song for Dov Shamir') or even an Egyptian lady during the reign of Amenhotep III (in 'A Faithful Wife').

J.C. The poem *Funland*, of course, is spoken by a madman.

D.A. Yes, by an inmate where the whole earth is a hospital, a mental hospital, endowed by Mr. Eliot's 'ruined millionaire.'

J.C. Because the one who speaks is an inmate of such a hosptial the poem does seem different from most of your poems, more dislocated.

D.A. I wrote some precursors to it in *A Small Desperation*. There's one poem in that volume that's by, as it were, one who'd had a nervous breakdown.

J.C. 'A Winter Convalescence'?

D.A. Right. And another poem, 'A Suburban Episode' is presented as being by one who's not merely neurotic but one more dissociated, with gradiose delusions. A psychotic. Since I'd written poems as a doctor I wanted to imagine poems by patients.

J.C. 'A Suburban Episode,' that's the poem that ends with a rock falling down an endless chasm. Let me find it . . .

> *Why, have I not heard, even I, first cousin*
> *of the mayor, heard in the night a stone falling?*

> *No ordinary stone either, scraping the sheer ledges,*
> *and later many stones, boulders even, leaping down*
> *out of earshot, down the sides of hell.*

'Funland' like 'A Winter Convalescence' and like 'A Suburban Episode' is not written with rhyme, or metrical or stanzaic regularity. Free verse, I suppose is apt for the chaotic minds of those who speak these poems.

D. A. We talked earlier about magical thinking. The crazy often think logically though they may start from an utterly absurd premise. Deluded they sometimes try to decode all kinds of things, find false significance in details.

J. C. Like when your protagonist in 'Funland' says:

> *All day mysterious aeroplanes*
> *fly over*
> *leaving theurgic vapour trails*
> *dishevelled by the wind*
> *horizontal chalky lines*
> *from some secret script*
> *announcing names perhaps*
> *of those about to die.*

D. A. I got that from the case history of Wilhelm Reich. You know towards the end of his life in Maine he went mad. He believed in those orgone-boxes, he believed he could make rain fall, that he could cure cancer. The F.B.I. began to investigate his activities. Then Reich, under pressure from them, observed the planes that happened to fly over. At once he decided that President Eisenhower had sent them—they were a secret signal from Eisenhower to him!

J. C. In 'Funland' power considerations and powerlessness are everywhere put before us. A scapegoat is needed so the blue-haired, red-eyed Thracians become the enemy.

D. A. I reversed Xenophanes' satirical remark about Thracians: how horses, if they could paint, would paint their gods in the shape of horses; oxen would paint them in the image of oxen; and Thracians, because they themselves had blue eyes and red hair made their gods

173

have blue eyes and red hair. The Nazis in Germany, by the way, painted Jesus as a blue-eyed aryan blond. Our sanity is precarious.

J.C. In *Pythagoras*, your main character—Pythagoras Smith—is a stage magician who goes mad, then believes himself to be the original Pythagoras reincarnated. He's a very appealing character. In 'Funland,' Pythagoras and the other characters you portray are silhouettes of those that you present in the play.

D.A. When you make characters in poems they tend to be one-dimensional. In plays, obviously, characters can react to and against each other, directly display their ambivalences and ambiguities, behave in a way that reveals their character. *Pythagoras*, of all the plays I've written is my favourite because, while not a verse-drama in the conventional sense, its language reaches towards poetic effect and, indeed, frequently relies on the metaphorical power of language.

J.C. In the poem 'Funland,' and in the play *Pythagoras*, related as they are, I'm made to feel, despite all the comedy you allow, the desolation and loneliness of the characters. I presume that came out in the production at Birmingham Rep.?

D.A. I think so, yes. And there was, I'm glad to say, much laughter in the theatre . . . Coleridge once remarked that 'Comedy is the blossom of the nettle.'

J.C. One scene I found particularly fascinating occurs when the patients are exhibited to the medical students. I felt as though I was one of those medical students. I was also repelled by the exploitation inherent in that arrangement. Do psychiatrists today, is it current practice, to demonstrate psychotic patients in that manner to medical students?

D.A. Yes they do. When I was a student at Westminster Hospital I went with others to a mental hospital and had patients demonstrated to us in very much the way I describe in *Pythagoras*. I've never forgotten one of the patients demonstrated. She seemed so sane. She began her peroration to the students saying that, of course, we must think her mad—else why was she there, and why speaking to us voluntarily right now? She was bored, she said, in the hospital, and to talk to us made life more interesting. Besides, she was a spiritualist—and she felt evangelical about her spiritualism as others were about other religions. So she could take this opportunity to try and convert us a little toward her viewpoint. She was reasonable, tidily dressed, pleasant to look at, smiling. After she left, the psychiatrist told us how, alas, one of her spirit-guides from time to time suggested she take a knife and murder someone, and that she tried to obey this spirit-guide.

J.C. In *Pythagoras* even the psychiatrist has some difficulty in distinguishing the sane from the insane. This implied critical view of the limitations of medical practice is present too in *The Dogs of Pavlov*, a play which I think is sustained both by its artistic consistency and its moral force. I'm surprised it didn't go into production in the West End.

D.A. It's not a comfortable play to sit through. When I saw it last produced in a small theatre in New York I didn't enjoy it as I do when I see *Pythagoras* performed. *The Dogs of Pavlov* is a violent play.

J.C. Like *Pythagoras* it shows how people are manipulated. But here the theme goes beyond the medical exploitation of people, beyond the human guinea-pig syndrome, to how people obey evil commands. Is the origin of your moral position to be found in the suffering in the Holocaust: in the fate of the Jews of Europe in the middle of this century? Do you write as a Jew? You once said in response to an enquiry in *The Jewish Quaterly* of winter 1964—that 'Auschwitz made you more of a Jew than ever Moses did.'

D.A. That's still true. And I sometimes find myself writing as a Jew—it is, I suppose, one component of my writing. Sometimes I'm forced by others or by circumstance or even by history to feel myself to be a Jew. For instance, the one and only occasion I went to Germany—I had to visit an R.A.F. hosptial at Wegberg—I needed to write a poem called 'No more Mozart.'

J.C. That's the poem that contains the lines:

> The German streets tonight
> are soaped in moonlight.
> The streets of Germany are clean
> like the hands of Lady MacBeth.

D.A. You may be amused to learn that 'No more Mozart' was recently translated into Hebrew and those lines then read:

> *The German streets tonight*
> *are soaped in moonlight.*
> *The streets of Germany are clean*
> *like the hands of Mrs. MacBeth.*

J. C. A number of Jewish writers in America—to name just two, Karl Shapiro and Bernard Malamud—have made explicit statements about the Jew being the symbol of the central victimised and alienated figure of our time . . .

D. A. . . . As this century continues more atrocities occur and recur in different parts of the world. Man has been a wolf to man irrespective of whether he's a Jew, a Christian or a Moslem. So that central symbol of the Jew is likely to become diluted. On the other hand, the crime against the Jews in war-torn Europe, the immensity of that crime cannot diminish, even in a small measure, in the minds of those who have truly apprehended it. For them, whatever other crimes against nations occur, nothing is annulled. That sickening apprehension has changed their minds forever, deepened their distrust in man.

J. C. Changed *your* mind forever, deepened *your* distrust?

D. A. Yes.

J. C. I asked you about the Jew being a symbol of the victimised figure of our time and you've answered me; but I also asked you about the Jew as being the alienated figure of our time. What about the title of your most recent book of poems?

D. A. *Way Out in the Centre?*

J. C. Yes.

D. A. Does that title suggest to you a geographical spiritual position?

J. C. It suggests to me that in a complicated way you think of yourself as being an Outsider.

D. A. It's a dualistic position. The title, after all, is a paradox. As you know I was born and brought up in Cardiff, a border town.

Though Cardiff's the capital of Wales, it's not very Welsh. One aspect of it faces West to Welsh Wales. One East to confident England. There are some who are scornful of such a mongrel city but out of the tensions of a double tradition a city may just as well be enriched as impoverished. So it is with its inhabitants. In my case, moreover, I'm a Jew—and to add to the complication one who's hardly part of the Jewish community.

J. C. You say that even though, in recent years, you've admitted that in writing your poems you've raided midrashic texts, legends of the bible.

D. A. Right. In recent poems of mine you'll find images I've stolen, images and aphoristic sayings from the Talmud. But one can be fired by Talmudic or Chasidic stories, even occasionally adapting them, and still feel isolated from the Jewish community at large.

J. C. You feel yourself to be a maverick.

D. A. If you like. All my life I've had an enduring feeling of being way out in the centre. When I left Cardiff I went, eventually, to Westminster Hospital to study medicine. And most of the students there, in my day, were ex-public school boys, and not a few had afterwards gone to Oxford or Cambridge. I went to a working-class Catholic school in Splott, Cardiff where I was taught by Christian Brothers.

J. C. A middle-class Welsh Jewish boy in a working-class Irish Catholic school.

D. A. Exactly. It was no way a classy establishment. Boys from there *never* went to Oxford or Cambridge. Only a small minority progressed to University. I hasten to add that I was happy enough at that school, mainly because I was interested in playing games, in cricket and rugby. But for the first lesson of the day, the religious lesson, I with a few Protestant lads was banished to another, empty classroom. I was way out in the centre there and at medical school. So it was, too, in the R.A.F. later. I was an officer but I was conscious, in the Mess, of not sharing my fellow officers' social and political views about occasions, ceremonies, and issues. I daresay that dualistic or paradoxical situation in which I've always found myself is common to most poets who live in a Philistine society. All the same, some poets may be made aware of being a maverick more than others.

177

J.C. Some of your feelings about being Way Out in the Centre inform your poems. And perhaps it leads you to be critical of those who thrive uncomplicatedly in the centre. For instance, in your poem, 'Tales of Shatz' you seem to be mildly critical of the modern-type English Jew who's more and more assimilated—the 'Baruch Levy who changed his name to Barry Lee / who moved to Esher, Surrey, / who sent his four sons—Matthew, Mark, Luke and John—to boarding school . . .' What you're doing here is what the prophets did in drawing attention to how Jews had moved away from their spiritual values.

D.A. That's much too grand. All I was trying to do in 'Tales of Shatz' was to catch the wry flavour you find in certain Yiddish stories. I don't know Yiddish but I admire in translation, such writers as Sholom Aleichem—their wryness, their humour, their humanity. That tone, that's what I was fumbling for in 'Tales of Shatz' and like Sholom Aleichem I hope I was affectionately satirical.

J.C. Your origins, as we know, apart from being Jewish are also Welsh. Your mother spoke Welsh, I believe.

D.A. Yes, when she was a young girl in Ystalyfera. As a matter of fact my grandmother, Annabella Shepherd spoke Welsh also. True, it was a broken Welsh, a peculiar Welsh, and the inhabitants of Ystalyfera—a village in the Swansea valley—wondered if she were a Patagonian. You see, in the 19th century, there'd been a Welsh settlement in Patagonia and no doubt when these Patagonians returned to Wales their Welsh was somewhat different to those who'd stayed behind. They used to say to my grandmother, because of her execrable Welsh—'Tell the truth, Annabella fach, you're not Jewish, you're Patagonian!'

J.C. Though I know you don't speak Welsh yourself, given your background, aren't you attracted to the *Matter* of Britain in the way you're attracted to the *Matter* of the Eastern European *shtetls*?

D.A. The early Welsh tradition was often focussed on the fabulous. The *Mabinogion*, for instance. I'm not excited by highly romantic Arthurian tales as I am by that component of the Jewish tradition that presents fallible characters recognisably, absurdly, human. I'm more interested in fools talking to their dogs than knights killing

178

dragons. Sometimes, of course, it's Welsh fools talking to Welsh dogs that intrigue me.

J. C. How should a poem declare itself to be Welsh?

D. A. Best of all by being written in Welsh—though there is such a thing as an Anglo-Welsh tradition.

J. C. I've noticed how many Anglo-Welsh poets, especially in recent years, plant an occasional Welsh word in their poems.

D. A. I don't scatter my poems with token Welsh. That would be a condescension. Almost one hundred years ago Emrys ap Iwan spoke satirically of those Welshmen who found it poetic to conclude each speech in English in barely tolerable Welsh, 'Long live the Welsh language.'

J. C. But you do have a strong sense of place.

D. A. Perhaps. For Ogmore-by-Sea where I think I was conceived, for Cardiff where I was born, for London which educated me, and for another place that has no name and you'll find on no map.

J. C. How do you mean?

D. A. It's something lost. It's not innocence, it's a form of know-ledge that is lost. It's more than 'hiraeth' which is an untranslatable Welsh word that has something to do with a longing for home, the yearnings of an exile for something lost. No, perhaps a Chasidic story best dramatises what I mean. May I quote it? It's a kind of parable.

J. C. Another parable?

D. A. I'm afraid so. 'When the Baal Shem had a difficult task before him, he would go to a certain place in the woods, light a fire and meditate in prayer—and what he had set out to perform was done. When a generation later the 'Maggid' of Meseritz was faced with the same task he would go to the same place in the woods and say: We can no longer light the fire, but we can still speak the prayers—and what he wanted done became reality. Again a generation later Rabbi Moshe Leib of Sassov had to perform his task. And he too went into the woods and said: We can no longer light a fire, nor do we know the secret meditations belonging to the prayer, but we do know the place in the woods to which it all belongs—and that must be

179

sufficient; and sufficient it was. But when another generation had passed and Rabbi Israel of Rishin was called upon to perform the task, he sat down on his golden chair in his castle and said: We cannot light the fire, we cannot speak the prayers, we do not know the place, but we can tell the story of how it was done.'

J.C. I like that. But it does strike a rather pessimistic note.

D.A. I wouldn't say that. It's a recognition of a loss but . . .

J.C. It has the same pessimism as 'Dover Beach.'

D.A. True 'Dover Beach' is a recognition that ignorant armies clash by night but it's also a prescription. For individuals on a personal level to be true to each other. And the parable, the Chassidic parable, prescribes that we must tell the story, must bear witness. The imperative for poets to bear witness is an old one. No doubt, one could find it in several cultures. The sixth-century bard, Aneurin, told us that of more than three hundred wearing gold torques at Catraeth only two returned from battle—one, Cibno, and the other, the bard himself, 'soaked in blood for my song's sake.'

J.C. Let me raise another question about *Way Out in the Centre*. I read a review recently which I'd like to quote from. Philip Owens wrote, 'It appears that the main problem these poems tackle is a substantial one—the question of how truth or reality is most accurately to be apprehended—and underlying it is a tension between two methods of approach (which we might define as the empirical and the imaginative) which, one presumes, emerges from the interplay of Abse's vocations as doctor and poet.' How do you feel about that?

D.A. Was that from *The Anglo-Welsh Review*?

J.C. Yes.

D.A. Many of my recent poems do seem to be about appearances, about what seems to be real, and how we may be deceived. There are those, I think, you're one, who wish to compartmentalise my occupations of doctor and poet. Oh there he's a doctor, here he's a poet. I don't think I'm that divided. Of course I have conflicts, tensions and I do contradict myself. In that, I'm like everybody else, and such oppositions within oneself do help to breed poems. Besides, though I start with the visible, I don't know where I'm going to end.

J. C. There are a number of poems in *Way Out* that are about different kinds of deception.

D. A. Right. There's a poem about vagrants but, imaginatively, are those down-and-outs what they seem? There's a poem about a door of a so-called haunted house banging and banging in the wind —how does one perceive that? There's a poem on how, looking out of a window four hoofmarks in the snow can be seen but suddenly these dark marks rise up like crows and fly away. At least three of them do.

J. C. What's particularly interesting is one dark mark remains behind!

D. A. That apprehension may only be a consequence of the optic nerve of the soul not yet having been severed!

J. C. To conclude, if I were to ask you to read a poem from *Way Out in the Centre* without thinking about the choice, which one would you turn to?

D. A. There's a poem of Amir Gilboa, the Israeli poet, I've adapted. About how we observe blood but we're told, officially, it's paint. With all the euphemisms and propaganda coming from the Middle East, at the moment, perhaps I could read his 'Lesson in Reality'?

> *They held up a stone.*
> *I said, 'Stone.'*
> *Smiling they said, 'Stone.'*
>
> *They showed me a tree.*
> *I said, 'Tree.'*
> *Smiling they said, 'Tree.'*
>
> *They shed a man's blood.*
> *I said, 'Blood.'*
> *Smiling they said, 'Paint.'*
>
> *They shed a man's blood.*
> *I said, 'Blood.'*
> *Smiling they said, 'Paint.'*

J. C. Thank you. Thank you very much.

SELECTED BIBLIOGRAPHY

Separate Works

After Every Green Thing. London: Hutchinson & Co., 1948.

Walking Under Water. London: Hutchinson & Co., 1952.

Ash On A Young Man's Sleeve. London: Hutchinson & Co., 1954; New York: Criterion Books, 1955, Second English edition: Oxford: Pergamon Press Ltd., 1969; Third edition: London: Valentine, Mitchell & Co., 1971, 1973; Fourth edition: London: Corgi Books, 1972; Fifth edition: London: Penguin Books Ltd., 1982; reprinted 1983.

Some Corner Of An English Field. London: Hutchinson & Co., 1956; New York: Criterion Books, 1956.

Tenants of the House: Poems 1951–1956. London: Hutchinson & Co., 1957; reprinted 1958; New York: Criterion Books, 1959.

Poems, Golders Green. London: Hutchinson & Co., 1962.

Three Questor Plays. London: Scorpion Press, 1967.

Medicine On Trial. London: Aldus Books, 1967; reprinted New York: Crown Publishers, 1969.

A Small Desperation. London: Hutchinson & Co., 1968.

O. Jones, O. Jones. London: Hutchinson & Co., 1970.

Selected Poems. London: Hutchinson & Co., 1970; reprinted 1971 and 1973; New York: Oxford University Press, 1970.

Funland And Other Poems. London: Hutchinson & Co., 1973; reprinted 1974; New York: Oxford University Press, 1973.

The Dogs of Pavlov. London: Valentine, Mitchell & Co., 1973.

A Poet In The Family. London: Hutchinson & Co., 1974.

Collected Poems 1948–1976. London: Hutchinson & Co., 1977; reprinted 1981; Pittsburgh: University of Pittsburgh Press, 1977.

Pythagoras. London: Hutchinson & Co., 1979.

Miscellany One. Bridgend: Poetry Wales Press, 1981.

Way Out in the Centre. London: Hutchinson & Co., 1981; reprinted Athens, Georgia, as *One Legged on Ice*: University of Georgia Press, 1983.

A Strong Dose of Myself. London: Hutchinson & Co., 1983.

Works Edited By Dannie Abse

Poetry And Poverty, Nos. 1–7. ed. Dannie Abse. London. 1949–1954; reprinted with *Mavericks* by Kraus Thomson Organization Ltd., Nendeln, Liechtenstein, 1968.

Mavericks. eds. Dannie Abse and Howard Sergeant. London: Editions Poetry And Poverty, 1957.

Modern European Verse. The Pocket Poets. ed. Dannie Abse. London: Vista Books, 1964.

Corgi Modern Poets in Focus: Nos. 1, 3 and 5. ed. Dannie Abse. London: Corgi Books 1971–1973.

Poetry Dimension Annual Nos. 2–7. ed. Dannie Abse. London: Robson Books Ltd., 1974–1980.

My Medical School. Ed. Dannie Abse. London. Robson Books Ltd. 1978.

Wales in Verse. Ed. Dannie Abse. London: Secker and Warburg, 1983.

Critical Essays on Dannie Abse

Roland Mathias. 'The Head Still Stuffed With Feathers': *The Anglo-Welsh Review*. Vol. 15 No. 36. Summer 1966.

John Smith. The Search for Identity: *Cahiers Franco-Anglais* No. 1 Poesie Vivante 1967.

Roland Mathias. 'The One Voice That is Mine'; *The Anglo-Welsh Review*. Vol. 16. No. 38, Winter 1967.

Jeremy Robson. 'Dannie Abse': *Modern Poets in Focus 4*. Corgi Books 1971.

Fleur Adcock. 'Poet on Poet.' *Ambit* 70. 1977.

Howard Sergeant. 'The Poetry of Dannie Abse': *Books and Bookmen*. July 1977.

John Pikoulis. 'Predicaments of Otherness': *Poetry Wales*. Vol. 13. No. 2 October 1977.

John Tripp. 'Dannie Abse Revisited': *Poetry Wales*. Vol. 13. No. 2 October 1977.

David Punter. 'Varieties of Defiance': *Straight Lines* No. 2 1979.

Glyn Jones. 'Dannie Abse': *Profiles*. Gomer Press, 1980.

Renee Winegarten. 'Dannie Abse: Vision and Reality': *Jewish Chronicle Literary Supplement*. Dec. 24th 1982.

Interviews in *The Jewish Quarterly* Winter 1963–64; *The Anglo-Welsh Review* Spring 1973; *The Guardian* January 31st, 1978; *Good Housekeeping* May 1981; *The Times* February 28th, 1983.

Notes on Contributors

Alan Brownjohn was educated at elementary and grammar schools in London, and at Merton College, Oxford. He has been a teacher in various kinds of school, a lecturer in a College of Education and Polytechnic, and is now a full-time writer. He has published seven volumes of poetry, the most recent being *A Night in the Gazebo* (Secker and Warburg, 1981, a Choice of the Poetry Book Society) and his *Collected Poems* have just been published by Secker. He has published a novel for teenagers, edited various anthologies and is a frequent contributor to BBC radio poetry programmes and to the main literary periodicals.

John Cassidy was born in Lancashire in 1928. He was an under-graduate and post-graduate student at Manchester University, and is now a lecturer at a tertiary college. His publications include *The Dancing Man* (Poet's Yearbook Award 1977), *An Attitude of Mind* (Hutchinson 1978), *The Fountain* and *Changes of Light* (Bloodaxe 1979) and *Night Cries* (Bloodaxe 1982, a Poetry Book Society Recommendation). His work has been frequently anthologised and broadcast, and he has reviewed for *Poetry Review*.

Joseph Cohen was born in 1926 and was educated at Vanderbilt University, Nashville, and the University of Texas, Austin, where he took his Ph.D degree in 1955. He is Professor of English and director of the Jewish Studies Program at Tulane University, New Orleans. He has published widely on the English poets of World War I and contemporary Anglo-American literature. His *Journey To*

184

The Trenches: The Life of Isaac Rosenberg, 1890–1918, appeared in 1975.

Donald Davie, born 1922 in Barnsley, Yorkshire, is Honorary Fellow of Trinity College Dublin and St Catharine's College, Cambridge. Since 1968 he has spent the greater part of most years in the USA, where he has honorary degrees from the University of Southern California and the University of the South. His *Collected Poems 1950–1970* appeared in 1972 from Routledge Kegan Paul, and his *Collected Poems 1971–1983* has just appeared from Carcanet Press. He is co-editor of *PN Review*. His memoirs, *These The Companions*, appeared last year from Cambridge University Press.

D. J. Enright was born in Leamington Spa in 1920. He has taught literature, mainly overseas, and more recently worked in publishing in London. He has edited *The Oxford Book of Contemporary Verse 1945–1980* (1980) and *The Oxford Book of Death* (1983). His *Collected Poems* appeared in 1981 (Oxford University Press), and his latest book is *A Mania for Sentences* (Chatto & Windus).

Barbara Hardy is Professor of English at Birkbeck College, University of London. Author of *The Novels of George Eliot* (1959 Athlone Press); *The Appropriate Form* (1964 Athlone Press); *Middlemarch: Critical Approaches to the Novel* (1967); *The Moral Art of Dickens* (1970 Athlone Press); *Radical Themes in Thackeray* (1972 Peter Owen); *Tellers and Listeners: The Narrative Imagination* (1975 Athlone Press); *Jane Austen* (1975 Peter Owen); *The Advantage of Lyric* (1977 Athlone Press); *Particularities: Readings in George Eliot* (1982 Peter Owen).

Daniel Hoffman, born in New York, N.Y. in 1923, is the author of seven books of poetry, most recently *Brotherly Love* (Random House, 1981). His *Able Was I Ere I Saw Elba: Selected Poems 1954–1974* (London: Hutchinson) appeared in 1977. He is the author also of several critical studies, including *Poe Poe Poe Poe Poe Poe Poe* (London: Robson Books, 1973). Daniel Hoffman was the 1973–74 Consultant in Poetry of the U.S. Library of Congress; he is Felix Schelling Professor of English Literature at the University of Pennsylvania.

Jeremy Hooker was born near Southampton in 1941 and has been a lecturer in the English department at the University College of Wales, Aberystwyth since 1965. From 1981–3 he was Arts Council creative writing fellow at Winchester School of Art. He has published six collections of poetry and critical studies of John Cowper Powys and David Jones, and he edited, with Gweno Lewis, *Selected Poems of Alun Lewis*. His own selected poems, *A View from the Source*, and a selection of essays and reviews, *Poetry of Place*, were published by Carcanet Press in 1982.

Gigliola Sacerdoti Mariani is full professor of English and teaches both at the University of Padua and the University of Florence, Italy. She has published books and essays on the language of Spenser's *Shepheardes Calendar*, on the English orthography of the sixteenth century, on the English lexicography of the seventeenth century, as well as on English and American literature. Her articles on George Eliot, Benjamin Disraeli, Virginia Woolf, Dannie Abse, Saul Bellow, Bernard Malamud, and Isaac Bashevis Singer have appeared in a variety of journals. She has contributed regularly to *Nuova Antologia*, one of the most prestigious journals of the humanities, politics and arts in Italy. She has introduced and translated a selection of Abse's poems in the annual collection of international poetry, *Almanaco dello Specchio*, published by Mondadori.

John Ormond was born in 1923 and was educated at Swansea Grammar School (where for a time he was taught English by Dylan Thomas's father) and at the University of Wales. As a young man he was a writer on Sir Tom Hopkinson's *Picture Post* and from 1955 until 1983 a writer and director of documentary films for the BBC. He has published various volumes of poetry, a selection being included in *Penguin Modern Poets 27*. He lives in Cardiff.

Peter Porter's recent *Collected Poems* was published by Oxford University Press. He was born in Brisbane, Australia, in 1929 and came to England in 1951. For two years recently he was writer-in-residence at Edinburgh University but he has now returned to London to work as a free-lance writer. He broadcasts regularly with the BBC and is also the main poetry reviewer for the *Observer*. At present he is preparing an *Oxford Book of Musical Verse*.

186

M. L. Rosenthal's latest book of poetry is his *Poems 1964–1980* (1981). His most recent books of criticism include *Poetry and the Common Life* (1974, 1983), *Sailing into the Unknown: Yeats, Pound, and Eliot* (1978), and *The Modern Poetic Sequence: The Genius of Modern Poetry* (1983–with Sally M. Gall). Professor of English at New York University, he has written for many British and American publications, has been Poetry Editor of *The Nation* and *The Humanist*, and is now Poetry Editor of *Present Tense*.

Vernon Scannell was born in 1922. He is a Fellow of the Royal Society of Literature, and the winner of the Heinemann Award for Literature 1962 and the Cholmondeley Poetry Prize 1974. Poems include *The Loving Game* (1975), *New and Collected Poems* (1980) and *Winterlude* (1982). Criticism includes *Edward Thomas* (1963) and *Not Without Glory: Poetry of the Second World War*.

Theodore Weiss was born in Reading, Pennsylvania, USA. He attended Muhlenberg College and Columbia University. Having taught at Bard College, the University of North Carolina, Yale University, MIT, and other institutions, for the past seventeen years he has been a professor of English and Creative Writing at Princeton University. With his wife Renee he has published and edited the *Quarterly Review of Literature* for forty years. He has published ten books of poetry, most recently a long poem *Recoveries*, and several books of criticism, the latest being *The Man from Porlock: Engagements, 1944–1981*.